Praise for *Living and Dying*

"David Ranney's is our best acco   s
turn to the factory and other work_   _ae seventies.
Reading in some parts like a novel, it introduces us to
a remarkable cast of working-class characters, while
offering a refreshingly critical look at his own experiences.
We get compelling views of factory work, including the
physical dangers and injuries that came with it, as well as
a better understanding of a range of New Left organizing
efforts. With the experience of a radical organizer and the
insights of a very good social scientist, Ranney writes with
particular sensitivity about race relations in the workplace."
—James R. Barrett, author of *History from the Bottom Up & the
Inside Out: Ethnicity, Race, and Identity in Working-Class History*

"Apart from its merits as literature—it made me laugh
and weep—Dave's account of and reflections upon his
experience working in the southeast Chicago/northwest
Indiana region is valuable to young activists for at least
three reasons: 1) It provides information about the nature
and significance of the point of production to a generation
that has no more knowledge of what it was like than
would a Martian. 2) It offers an example of persistence
to a generation that tends to measure commitment in
days or weeks rather than years or a lifetime. 3) It shows
the possibility of personal transformation, both in those
like Dave who set out consciously to change the world
and in those he met in the course of his efforts to do
so—transformation, which is, after all, the whole point."
—Noel Ignatiev, author of *How the Irish Became White*

"David Ranney has produced a riveting memoir of his years working industrial jobs on the southeast side of Chicago. Compellingly written and thought provoking, *Living and Dying on the Factory Floor* brings to life the daily realities of race, class, and gender in an urban community on the brink of joining the rust belt. Ranney pairs vivid depictions of everyday forms of social struggle with timely reflections on the political implications for contemporary readers. This book will be required reading for the next generation of radicals, particularly those hoping to understand how we arrived at the postindustrial 'gig economy,' and how we dismantle it and construct a truly free society."

—Michael Staudenmaier, author of *Truth and Revolution: A History of the Sojourner Truth Organization, 1969–1986*

Living and Dying on the Factory Floor

From the Outside In and the Inside Out

David Ranney

Contents

Preface

And you may find yourself living in a shotgun shack.
And you may find yourself in another part of the world.
And you may find yourself behind the wheel of a large automobile.
And you may find yourself in a beautiful house with a beautiful wife.
And you may ask yourself, well how did I get here!?
—Talking Heads, "Once in a Lifetime"

I find myself sitting at my desk in a rural town in Northeastern Wisconsin looking at chickadees, nuthatches, and chipping sparrows diving in and out of the feeding stations I have set up for my amusement. Indigo buntings, purple finches, and many of the other birds have left for the winter. Suddenly a flock of juncos sails in and begins pecking at the ground beneath the feeders. They come in early spring and leave for the summer, and then stop by in the late fall and leave again for the winter. *How is it determined who goes and who stays? How do they mobilize and decide to wing their way from here to there?* From their perspective I am on the outside looking in. Yet I feel a connection. As I put up the feeders and keep them full of seeds and suet, many of the regulars sit on or near the feeders chirping happy sounds at me. At this moment, I feel like I'm sitting on the inside, looking out at their world.

I am suddenly interrupted from this reverie by an annoying ding from my cellphone. It is a CNN news alert about yet another presidential tweet. In this one the president claims that his proposed tax reform will bring "middle-class jobs" back to the U.S. For some reason this really sets me off. Feeling angry and agitated, my mind goes back forty years to a time when I was working in a number of factories in Southeast Chicago. It was another time in my life, one when I was both an outsider looking into the world of the factory workers and an insider looking out at the outside world.

I realized that the perspective I gained then is still with me today and accounts for my anger at the simplistic notion of "bringing back middle-class jobs." So I began to write about that time in my life, not as a memoir but as an account of life and even death on the factory floor, the raw class and race relations, the exploitation of backbreaking and dangerous labor, and the often unhealthy and unsafe working conditions. Sharing that perspective with others today seems timely and important.

In 1973, I was comfortably employed as a tenured professor at the University of Iowa in Iowa City. It was a time of great optimism and hope that we could replace a society based on greed, sexism, racism, and wars aimed at global domination with something new. I strongly believed, and still do, that we can achieve a totally new society in which "the full and free development of every human being is its ruling principle." It would be a society where the measure of wealth would be, in Marx's words, "the needs, capacities, enjoyments, and creative abilities" of each individual.

As these ideas were forming in Iowa City in the early 1970s, I was highly involved in local political and social activities, including opposition to the Vietnam War, supporting the demands of various civil rights groups, critiquing the political outlook of textbooks used in major survey courses at the University of Iowa, and experimenting with new social forms by organizing cooperative daycare, food co-ops, and housing co-ops. I helped to develop community education events about both the Vietnam War and the Southern African wars for national liberation from colonial powers. The political work and political education were intense and productive, but I increasingly began to feel that we were operating in a bubble that didn't really extend beyond Iowa City. I longed to engage the growing social justice and revolutionary movements all over the world and couldn't really do so from my comfortable perch.

So I took a one-year leave of absence and moved to Chicago, following my Iowa City friend Kingsley, who had opened up a unique pro bono legal clinic he called the Workers' Rights Center in a storefront office in Southeast Chicago. Initially I joined a socialist group called New American Movement (NAM) and worked in its national office but later joined the Sojourner Truth Organization (STO) and began working with Kingsley in the Workers' Rights Center.

By this time my one-year leave of absence at the University of Iowa had run out and so had my money. I made the difficult decision to leave academia. Many left-wing organizations, STO included, had members working in factories for a variety of reasons. STO believed, for reasons I will discuss at the end of this book, that a new society could be built from the initiatives of "mass organizations at the workplace." So it made sense that my financial needs could best be met by working in Southeast Chicago factories. The work was consistent with STO priorities and also engaged the sort of people who were coming to the Workers' Rights Center for legal help. This is how I came to work at a number of different factories from 1976 to 1982.

The area I worked in during this period, Southeast Chicago and Northwest Indiana, included one of the largest concentrations of heavy industry in the world. The region was anchored by ten steel mills, which, at their peak, employed two hundred thousand workers, half in Chicago. It has been estimated that for every steel job in the region there were seven other manufacturing workers, bringing the total employment to over one-and-a-half-million workers. The presence of the Lake Michigan ports, rivers that served industry, railroad spurs, highways, and the mills themselves attracted firms that manufactured steel products like automobiles, railroad cars, and steel structures. It also attracted industries that supplied products to the mills and to other factory workers—chemicals, processed food, tools, work boots, welding equipment. Today, nearly all of this is gone. All the Chicago steel mills have been closed and demolished, along with most of the firms whose location was determined by the mills. There is still as much steel produced in Northwest Indiana but by a fraction of the workers. In terms of just steelworkers, there are less than ten thousand left, and that number is declining. What the mills and heavy industry left behind is toxic waste and crushing poverty.

The seven factories I worked in during the late 1970s and early 1980s were not steel mills but represented a fair cross section of what factory work once was like on a day-to-day basis. This history is important, because it exposes the negative class and race relations that persist. It also shows how such relations could and do change when working people confront a common threat and a promise of something better. It exposes the threats to worker health and safety that are inherent in these jobs. And it exposes the legacy of environmental decay that is still with us.

What follows are my experiences written in story form without any analysis or explanation of why I was working on the factory floor. The focus is on the day-to-day working conditions of the people I worked with and the experiences we shared. I have written these stories in real time (present tense) and from my point of view at that time (first-person). In the final section of the book I reflect on why I did this, how it worked out for me, and how my experience can be useful for determining a direction forward today.

1976–1977: You'll Get Used to It

I t is my first day at the Workers' Rights Center. I leave my new apartment at 8:00 a.m. and make my way to Commercial Avenue. It is a vibrant strip of bars, restaurants, and all sorts of shops, including a supermarket and a large variety "Dollar Store." Many of the bars and restaurants are open and filled with workers coming off of their shifts at the steel mill and neighborhood factories that run around the clock. Commercial Avenue is full of people entering and leaving the bars and restaurants or on their way to or from work. The diversity of Southeast Chicago's working-class population is on permanent display—Eastern Europeans, blacks, and Mexicans mingle freely on Commercial Avenue but live in distinct, effectively segregated areas of the Southeast Side of Chicago. There is also a lot of automobile, truck, and bus traffic that creates a continual din of motors and horns. As I approach the office, the air is thick with the fumes of nearby U.S. Steel Southworks, motor vehicle exhaust, and an as yet unidentified unpleasant odor of another plant in the vicinity. The odor reminds me of once cooking french fries after a rat or a mouse had died in the walls of our kitchen.

The air is gritty. I look at cars parked along Commercial Avenue and notice that they are coated with a fine red dust. I run my finger over one of the cars and consider writing a political message on it. That seems juvenile, so I wipe the dust off my finger onto my jeans. Everything seems to be covered by the red dust.

Near the Workers' Rights Center is a huge cathedral, Immaculate Conception, built in the nineteenth century. I stop to read a sign in front of the church that announces the times of masses in English, Spanish, and Polish. Looking east down 88th Street I see a number of other churches—another Roman Catholic cathedral and some smaller

Baptist churches that Kingsley tells me serve the community's black population.

I turn left on 88th Street and arrive at the Workers' Rights Center, at mid-block. It is a walk-in pro bono (free) legal clinic that is mostly involved with immigration rights, worker conflicts in some of the area factories, and helping workers get their unemployment benefits when they are laid off.

I have no real legal training other than a few legal research courses when I was a graduate student at Syracuse University and my experience doing cross-examination with the Dartmouth debate team. So I assist Kingsley, doing what would be called paralegal work today. All the work we do is financed through Kingsley's personal funds and my savings from when I was a college professor. We advertise our services with flyers. Employers are routinely challenging laid-off workers who have filed for unemployment compensation. We let it be known that we can help these workers.

My first assignment with the Worker's Rights Center is to represent a worker at an unemployment compensation hearing. The administrative officer, who is employed by the State of Illinois, holds a hearing in a small conference room in a nondescript government building in the neighborhood. The worker and I enter the room and are asked by the officer to sit at a long conference table. The company representative then comes in and sits across from us. My client recognizes the man and looks down at the table. I can see that he is angry and intimidated by the sight of the company man. The company man speaks first, alleging that my client has been fired "for cause." He had been insubordinate, came late for work regularly, and was incapable of doing the work he had been hired to do. If these things hold up, the worker will face a six- to eight-week delay in gaining his benefits. At the low pay he was getting on the job, this would be a disaster for him and his family.

Here is roughly how the rest of the hearing went.

Me: "Isn't it true that my client has worked for you for two years?"
Company man: "Yes, that's true."
Me: "And all this insubordination, tardiness, and incompetence—when did that start happening?"
Company man: "It went on the whole time; we have just had enough."

Me: "Did you ever give him warnings."

Company man: "Yes, many times."

Me: "In writing?"

Company man: "Err . . . no."

Me: "No written warnings?"

Company man: "No. We treat our workers like family."

Me: "Actually, you have laid off a number of workers in the past month because sales are down and you don't want your unemployment taxes to go up. Isn't that right? How many workers have you laid off in the past month, and how many compensation claims have you challenged?"

Company man: "None of your business."

The administrator is shuffling through some files. She looks up. "It is my business, sir. I am awarding this employee immediate compensation."

Well, that was that. We have a number of similar victories. But we soon learn that even when awarded compensation, workers are not getting checks and are being given the runaround. We contact workers who had complained to us about this, as well as other unemployed clients, and call a meeting, asking them to bring papers documenting their unemployment compensation award. At the meeting one person after another tells of long lines, hours of waiting, a grilling about their efforts to find work, and a runaround once they get to talk to one of the clerks. We decide on the spot to march to the office and demand action. It is located about a quarter of a mile down 88th Street.

We prepare and distribute a short leaflet explaining what we are doing and why. We call several TV stations and tell them there will be a demonstration at the Stony Island office in two hours. We then start marching to the office, passing out leaflets along the way.

As we approach the office, we see a line of people stretching down the street. We pass out leaflets to those in line, explaining that we intend to occupy the offices and invite them to join us. Many do. We go inside. There is a long counter separating unemployed workers from State of Illinois employees. One bored looking worker behind the counter is talking to someone. There is a large open area behind the counter where other workers are sitting at desks, talking on the phone, and shuffling papers. At the end of the counter is a gate that opens a passage between

3

the two sections of the building. There are two security guards milling around.

We catch them by surprise, open the counter gate, and pour into the large inner sanctum. We then sit down. The guards and a supervisor order us to leave. We produce another leaflet stating that we will not leave until everyone is told in writing when they can expect their checks. Soon the television cameras and reporters arrive and so do the police. The police order us to leave. We continue to sit. The person in charge of the office comes out and tries to reason with us. Then she returns to her private office, reappearing about ten minutes later. She orders her employees to collect names. They then process all the claims. We stay until everyone has been promised a check within a week. We let her know that if they don't get their checks, we will be back with even more people. The tactic seems to work.

Eventually, my savings begin to dry up. My wife Beth has a clerical job, but her income is not enough to pay the bills for both of us. So she, Kingsley, and I decide that I will try to get work in one of the nearby factories. Many left groups are sending members into the factories to organize workers. This is not the case with me. But the three of us believe that my work in local factories might give the Workers' Rights Center more connection to the neighborhood. It is also a way to make needed money. But part of my decision involves a bit of bravado on my part and a romanticism of factory work itself.

I take my money woes and bravado to the employment offices of a number of local factories. The trouble is I have absolutely no skills or experience that would prepare me for factory work. An Ivy League education, a PhD, and experience as a college professor won't do and would certainly raise the suspicions of any potential employer. So I toss out my résumé and invent a work history.

A friend of mine in Cleveland agrees that while I am in the job market she will answer her phone "Prime Manufacturing." I also line up friends to represent themselves as a roofing company and a print shop. Only the print shop is real. I had done some work there printing political leaflets and pamphlets. If someone were to call checking my references they all agree to tell the story I have concocted about my work experience.

My first job is in a small "job shop" in East Chicago, Indiana, called FAROC. I never did figure out where the name came from. I saw an ad in a local newspaper, the *Daily Calumet*. What caught my eye were the words, "No prior experience required." To get there I have to drive onto the Chicago Skyway—a massive bridge that goes over Southeast Chicago's industrial heartland. From the Skyway I can see miles of bungalow homes, smaller and larger factories, and two steel mills, all going full tilt. As I get near East Chicago the acrid smell of steel production gets even stronger than it is in South Chicago. Smoke fills the air and visibility is limited. Massive integrated steel mills, including Inland Steel and U.S. Steel Gary Works, run around the clock. One of the operations in these mills is burning coal to make a product called coke that burns hot enough to combine limestone and iron into steel. There are also huge mills that use the raw steel to produce sheets, beams, tubes, and rails. Other factories nearby use steel to make blast furnaces and giant ladles that are needed for the steelmaking process. At one point, five steel mills in the area employed over one hundred thousand workers.

FAROC does something quite different. It is nestled in between the mills among hundreds of small shops doing a variety of kinds of work. I have a hell of a time even finding it. I get to the address given to me when calling to set up an interview. Finally, I spy a small sign on the door of a building that simply says "FAROC."

I enter the nondescript building for my interview. Inside the door, the entire shop floor can be seen. It is the size of about two football fields. There are roughly twenty workers doing various tasks. Some are welding steel strips on large pieces of machinery that look like giant corkscrews. In other parts of the plant, workers are using cranes to pull the corkscrew-like parts out of large cylinders. One cylinder is being loaded onto a flatbed truck by crane. In another location a worker is chipping away debris inside one of the cylinders, while another worker is pressure washing another cylinder. There are various metal shop machines here and there. One I recognize as a drill press. I haven't a clue what the others are. The noise of grinding and hammering is deafening. The smell is overpowering, reminiscent of the unpleasant odor around the Workers' Rights Center.

There is a small office in the back of the shop. A man appearing to be in his sixties stands in the doorway. He is thin, about six feet tall, wearing tinted safety glasses, a white shirt, and a stained tie. His face is heavily wrinkled, and he has a perpetual scowl, as if a smile would crack that face wide open. I look around uncertainly. I can feel my hands sweating and my stomach churning. *What am I getting myself into?*

The man motions me to approach with his head. "What do you want?"

"To apply for a job."

He motions me into the office. There is a calendar on the wall with a picture of a scantily clad young woman holding a wrench while standing in a suggestive pose. (This sort of soft porn used to be known as a "pin-up.") There is also a desk piled with papers and two chairs. The man gives me an application form. "Sit down and fill this out."

I sit and fill out the form with my phony work record and hand it to him. He glances at the form. "Be here tomorrow at 8:00 a.m. You will need to bring your own tools. Here's a list of the tools you will need." He hands me a list. "You'll start at $4.65 an hour and get raised to $5.00 in a month if you make it through probation. One of the men out there will tell you what to do."

"What do you make here?"

"Nothing. We rebuild centrifuge machines."

Centrifuge machines?! I reply, "Oh. Okay then and thanks. See you tomorrow."

He gives me a blank stare by way of a reply, and I leave the office and walk across the shop floor, nodding to the workers who are watching me. On my way home, I stop at Sears to buy the needed tools. The list is long. I am not sure what some items even look like, let alone how to use them. They include wrenches, both metric and standard: combination wrenches, adjustable wrenches, pipe wrenches, torque wrenches and a set of sockets, as well as hex keys, various kinds of hammers, and pry bars.

As I step into the Sears tool department I feel bewildered, scared, and a little depressed. I hand a helpful and eager clerk the list. He sells me a whole tool set, complete with toolbox. They are all shiny and new with a slight oil smell to them. I also pick up a lunch box in a separate department and some work clothes similar to what I had seen the other workers wearing.

The next morning, I leave our apartment at 7:00 a.m. It took me forty minutes to drive the day before. But Skyway traffic today is backed up. Once off the Skyway I have to cross two lift bridges to get to East Chicago. Both bridges are up letting ships through this morning, causing more traffic backups. I am feeling agitated and in a bad mood that is tempered by being scared shitless when I arrive at 8:30—a half hour late the first day of my new life at the point of production.

I walk into the plant and the same mean-looking boss is standing in the door to his office. If I were about to go on stage in the theater my physical feelings would be called "stage fright." But what do I call this? My adrenalin seems to be gushing, and I feel like I have massive butterflies flapping around in my stomach. I walk up to the boss.

"Sorry I'm late. I didn't know the bridges would be up at this time of the morning."

He hands me a time card with my name on it. "Punch in there and put your card in the rack. You'll be docked for the half hour. Don't come late again."

He takes me over to one of the workers who appears to be about forty years old, the oldest of the workers I can see. He is white (I realize that all the workers there are white), thin but wiry, and is wearing safety glasses, work boots, and a dark blue shirt and pants identical to those I purchased at Sears. His clothes and boots are stained and worn and mine are shiny and new.

"Bob, this is Dave. Show him what to do." He then turns and walks back into his office and shuts the door.

We shake hands. We have to shout to be heard over the noise. "He's a real prick," he yells. "In fact that is what we call him when he is out of range, but you'll get used to him. Isn't this a lovely place?"

I glance nervously at the office.

"He can't hear any better than the rest of us. The noise gives us our privacy."

He looks at my toolbox. "Oooh, new tools!" He then looks me over and smirks: "And a brand-new set of clothes. Sears, right? He takes my toolbox and sets it on a table, opens it, and paws through its contents.

I feel myself blushing. "My old tools were stolen," I stammer.

He laughs. "Okay, you can use my tools if you don't have what you need."

I do not want to appear as ignorant as I am but need to trust someone to a degree to figure out how to do stuff. Bob is the only option. "I've never worked in a place like this. The 'prick' says you rebuild centrifuges. I've never heard of them. What do they do?"

Bob laughs. He has a low-key easy laugh. "Don't worry about it. Very few people know what a centrifuge is. Basically, the thing that looks like a corkscrew is called a conveyer. It goes inside the cylinder and spins at a high rate of speed. It separates liquids from solids. The conveyer pushes the solid stuff out one end and the liquid comes out of the other, kinda like shit and piss."

"What kind of stuff?"

He laughs again. "Now this is the good part. These are used for a lot of things but most of the machines we rebuild here come from the rendering plants. They boil dead pigs, cows, horses, or what have you, and the resulting nasty mash is fed into the centrifuge. The solid shit is thrown away; God knows where. The liquids are separated and made into various things. Like I said, kinda like shit and piss. For real. The pig fat and cow fat end up in your basic cookies and pies. Spinning all that stuff eventually wears out the conveyor and puts the whole machine out of balance. Basically, what we do is clean the shit out of everything, build up the conveyer with new steel, rebalance both the conveyer and cylinder with steel weights, put in new bearings and gaskets, put the sucker back together, and take it back to the rendering plant. Ever been to a rendering plant? If you think this place stinks, you ought to get the prick to let you help with a delivery."

"I'm not that curious. It sounds like it would be easier if they just bought a new centrifuge."

"Then you wouldn't have a job," he laughed.

Bob takes me around and introduces me to the other workers. We end up where one of the workers is starting to take apart a centrifuge that has just come in. "This is Ken, and this is Dave. Dave is on probation so don't let him fuck up."

I look at the tools Ken is using and grab some hex keys, a hammer, and a pry bar from my toolbox. The cylinder is sitting vertically. We use step ladders to reach a lid that is screwed to one end. We begin taking the screws out. At some point we attach a hook to the lid we are removing. The lid is about four feet in diameter. The hook is then attached to a cable on a crane that runs along a beam on the ceiling. We tighten the cable slightly and remove the final screws. Then we pry the lid off and lift it slightly with the crane, move it clear of the cylinder, and slowly lower it to the ground. As we do this, the smell is so bad I gag.

Ken stares at me, and I say, "I'm glad I'm not a homicide detective or a rendering worker."

Ken laughs. "Yeah, pretty bad. You'll get used to it though."

"Bob said that about our boss."

"That's more difficult. We call him 'the prick.'"

I use a flashlight to look inside the cylinder. We are clearly at the solids end. I can see teeth and hair embedded in what looks like the dried cow shit that was ubiquitous in Calcutta when I lived there. I think I catch sight of a boiled ear. We begin chipping at the dried solids with our chisels and hammers until we loosen the conveyor a bit. We then use the crane to pull the conveyor straight out. By lunch time we have taken most of the centrifuge apart.

At 12:30, a bell rings. There is a washroom next to the boss's office—just a few toilets and a sink. We stand in line to take a leak and wash up. Then we go out to a corner of the shop floor and sit on a few benches to eat our lunches. I have packed a PB&J sandwich, a carrot, and a bottle of pop. I have to force myself to eat. I look up and the other guys are looking at me laughing.

"I know. I'll get used to it."

So my life as a factory worker begins.

I begin to get to know the other workers. One of them is always assigned the dirtiest job—cleaning. He is mentally challenged and a very sweet man. He never complains, even though some of the other workers and "the prick" make fun of him. He is a big man but very gentle. The character of Lenny in Steinbeck's *Grapes of Wrath* comes to mind. I wonder if he has a violent side. A number of people would have it coming if he ever erupted. But he doesn't during the time I work at FAROC.

One night when I am leaving the plant, I have a flat tire. I open the trunk to get the jack and spare. Ken stops to help. I realize that the trunk is full of leaflets advocating Puerto Rican independence and freedom for Puerto Rican nationalist political prisoners. Ken picks a leaflet up and reads it. He says nothing about it as he lifts the spare tire out while I jack up the car and remove the flat tire. He puts the flat tire back in the trunk and helps me lift the spare onto the car. Then he goes back and shuts the trunk, and we finish bolting the tire on. When we are finished:

"Thanks Ken."

"I'm with Workers World. Who are you with?"

"Sojourner Truth Organization. Fifteen guys working here and two are commies. Who would have guessed? Any more?"

"Not that I know of."

"Well thanks and let's Free the Five Puerto Rican Prisoners of War! Why not try to recruit the prick? Workers World can have him."

Ken laughs, and we go our separate ways. Politics never comes up again.

In the following months I am assigned to a variety of different jobs. I learn how to replace bearings, balance the conveyer, and fabricate weights and small parts. There are difficult moments, however.

★

Bob asks me to drill some three-eighth-inch holes into a small part that is being rebuilt. I go to the drill press, find a three-eighth-inch bit, and try to drill the hole while holding the piece with my hand. The entire piece spins around and scrapes the top of my hand making a large gash. I am bleeding. Bob comes over with a first aid kit and helps me patch it up.

"When you do that, use one of these little vices." He hands one to me. I feel stupid but nothing else is said. Bob knows better than anyone that I have no industrial experience. *Well the ad said, "No prior experience required."*

A few weeks later I am asked to use the big crane that runs along a beam in the middle of the shop to lift and load a finished centrifuge onto the bed of the delivery truck. I have never used a crane like this before. It is much larger than the little ones we use to take the machines apart. I have watched other workers do this and know how to use belts to rig the centrifuge for lifting. There is a handheld control: two buttons for up and down and two more to move the lifted centrifuge to a forklift that will take it to the truck parked outside.

I lift the centrifuge much too fast and it begins to swing wildly, like a bull coming out of the gate at a rodeo. Everyone scatters to get out of the way. I drop the controls and run for cover myself. Suddenly the crane breaks loose and hurtles the runaway centrifuge across the plant. It stops with a jolt once it reaches the end of the shop. If anyone had been in the way they would be dead. I am seriously shaken. I can see the prick standing in the doorway shaking his head. Bob comes up to me and gives me a little hug around the shoulders. "It happens. No one's hurt. Don't worry about it. Take it a little slower next time."

★

I don't get fired for the runaway crane incident. Actually, the crane was defective. But a few months later, my last day at this East Chicago shop, coincides with my first industrial accident. It is Saturday night. We are working overtime, which is unusual, but we have a rush job. There are many hazards in the shop. One is caused by the fact that we are never given the time to clean up properly after a job is finished. Consequently, there are pallets of parts and motors lying in aisleways (a federal government Occupational Safety and Health Administration violation no doubt). Tools are sitting around everywhere and the place is filthy.

I have mastered the crane and I am once again moving a finished centrifuge slowly toward a waiting forklift. As I am watching the moving machine, I step on a loose ball bearing that is sitting on the floor. The bearing is small; it is like a one-inch steel marble. I lose my balance, pitching backward onto the floor and hitting my head on a piece of metal sitting with old parts on a pallet. One of the workers comes over and helps me up. I am dizzy and can feel warm liquid on my face. I put my hand over my eye. There is blood, lots of blood. Bob has a clean rag and presses it over my eye. "Put pressure on it."

We go into the office. The prick takes one look at me and makes a new face (like something smelled bad?) "For Christ sake, what did you do this time?"

"Fell."

"You'll have to go to the goddamn hospital and get stitched up. Get going. I'll punch you out."

Bob: "I'll take him."

"The hell you will. We need to finish this job tonight. He's okay. Just needs a few stitches."

Me: "Err, where's the hospital?"

"Bob will give you directions."

Bob walks with me to my car and gives me directions. "Once again, the prick lives up to his name! You sure you're okay to drive?"

"I'll manage."

Bob has put a piece of tape across the gash on my forehead and has tied the rag around my head. I look like one of those guys in the drum, pipe, and bugle corps during the revolutionary war—the guy with the rag tied around his head. I drive to the emergency room entrance, park the car, and walk in. I am feeling a bit woozy. I walk up to the desk. I can see people sitting around a waiting area who look far worse off than me.

At least one guy is bleeding from his gut. *A knife wound?* Some are lying on gurneys.

"You the guy who fell at the machine shop? Your boss called."

"That's me."

"Who brought you over here?"

"Me."

She gives me a funny look. "Hmmpf! I'd look for another job if I were you. Sit over there. We're having a busy night. We'll get to you as soon as we can."

I sit for about three hours. At some point I use the phone at the intake desk to call Beth and let her know what's going on. Around midnight a nurse comes to me.

"Let's take a look at that." She takes the rag off my head. It and my shirt are soaked with blood. "Probably about six stitches will do it."

She guides me to a nearby gurney where I finally get to lie down. She then takes me into an area defined by the white curtain around it and leaves. A young guy in hospital scrubs comes in with the nurse (*a doctor? who knows?*). He has the equipment he needs to patch me up. I am out of there at 12:30 a.m. and driving home across the bridges and the skyway. The smoke is still pouring out of Inland Steel. The worker bungalows are mostly dark, but all the mills are as bright as day.

Since the next day is Sunday I have a bit of a respite. I go to work as usual on Monday. When I get there the prick is holding my time card. "You're not working out here. You're fired."

"That's illegal, you know—to fire a guy because he is hurt on the job?"

"I'm firing you because you are not worth a shit. Sue me!"

So ends my first foray onto the factory floor. I lasted only five months at this dirty little machine shop.

★

I go into the Workers' Rights Center that afternoon and tell Kingsley what happened.

"It was illegal," Kingsley says. "Want to contest it?"

"No. There are only fifteen workers there, and one is with Workers World. I think I'll try to find something else."

Just then a half dozen black men in their twenties come in the door. They tell us that they work at U.S. Steel Southworks and are forming a black caucus at the mill. They feel that they are getting screwed not only by the bosses but by the union as well. They just want help printing leaflets and to use the phone occasionally. We are located near the main gates of the mill. We offer to pass the leaflets out. And we discuss with them what we know of the union and company and tell them a little about the Workers' Rights Center.

There are other things bringing people into the Workers' Rights Center. Anti-immigrant feeling against Mexicans is high, and there is an ongoing push to deport Mexican workers without papers and work permits. Factories are being raided by the U.S. Immigration and Naturalization Service with the help of local police. La Migra, as they are called by Mexicans, surround factories, enter and check documents of workers who look Latino, arrest those who do not have documentation, and rapidly deport them to Mexico. People are even being stopped on the street by Migra agents.

The National Lawyers Guild, an organization of left-wing lawyers that Kingsley belongs to, begins a "know your rights" campaign. We distribute leaflets in Spanish and English that advise what to do if you are stopped on the street or arrested in your workplace. The leaflet includes lawyers' phone numbers. We distribute these at plant gates and on the street. On Saturday afternoons we enter Spanish language movie theaters with Mexican immigration rights activists. The manager of the Gayety Theater in South Chicago agrees to stop the film and turn on the lights and allow us to speak about immigration rights. I work with others distributing the National Lawyers Guild leaflet and also collect contributions from people in the theater to offset the costs of the campaign.

In support of this effort, the Workers' Rights Center takes an effective educational initiative. A comrade, Noel Ignatiev, has written a pamphlet called "Since When Has Working Been a Crime." It is aimed at black and white workers. The object is to promote class solidarity with Latino workers threatened by La Migra. The pamphlet tells the story of the Fugitive Slave Law of 1850 and compares the abduction of escaped slaves in the North to the Migra raids today. It also gives examples of resistance from that time. The point of the pamphlet is that it is in the interest of all workers to participate in the resistance to the 1970s version of the Fugitive Slave Acts. The Workers' Rights Center distributes the pamphlet to workers in the neighborhood.

1977–1978: There Ain't No Justice . . . Just Us

I quickly find a new job at a box factory owned by Mead Packaging Corporation. The plant makes cartons for soda and beer. A huge printing press prints the design on sheets of cardboard. The last station at the press is a stamping machine that cuts and folds the boxes that will be turned into carrying containers for six-packs. My job is to take the boxes as they come off the press and stack them on a skid. There are a number of us working on this. When my skid is full I grab a forklift and move the skid to an area where other workers are wrapping skids with shrink-wrap and moving them to the shipping docks. When I get back with my forklift it is my turn to take the boxes off the giant machine. It is backbreaking work. Occasionally we get welcome relief when the press breaks down and mechanics descend upon it to get it running again.

On the last day of my probation I am called into the plant manager's office about ten minutes before the end of my shift. He tells me he had a call from the corporation headquarters and has been instructed to let me go.

"I can't understand this. You work hard and have been reliable. I told them this and argued for keeping you. They said no. They're doin' background checks these days. Something turned up that upset someone. Any idea what this is about?"

"No clue," I answer.

He hands me a check and I walk out the door. I am relieved. There is no way I could have lasted doing that kind of work. I was hoping that they might train me to be a mechanic or even a press operator. But short of that . . .

I get back to the Workers' Rights Center. Kingsley tells me of an article in one of the leftie papers that reports that Mead had a strike in another city supposedly led by Trotskyists. I call my Cleveland friend. They had checked my references and really grilled her. I wonder what else they checked? I ask her if she is willing to keep at it. She says, "No problem." I'm back in the job market.

★

A few weeks later I come across an ad in a community paper, the *Daily Calumet*. There is an opening for a maintenance mechanic at a plant about five blocks from the office.

"Ever hear of Chicago Shortening? It's on 91st and Baltimore."

"Can't picture it," Kingsley replies. "Isn't there a YMCA over there?"

"I'm going to check it out."

"Good luck!"

I open the door to the office and go out onto the street. It is about 1:00 p.m. on a hot summer day. The acrid smell of smoke from U.S. Steel Southworks dominates the senses. There is that other smell as well that seems to work its way through the exhaust fumes of cars and trucks and the smoke from the mill. I realize that it reminds me of the smell of the shop floor at FAROC. I walk up 88th Street to Commercial. The noise of traffic, including horns and cars in need of new mufflers, is dominant. The streets, as usual, are bustling with people.

I turn the corner at 91st and walk east. Baltimore is two more blocks. I can see the YMCA, a relatively modern looking brick structure. It sits in sharp contrast to the older grimy and dilapidated industrial buildings around it. As I get nearer the YMCA I can see a nondescript brick factory building just beyond it. I notice that the unpleasant odor that was competing with the mill and car exhaust is getting stronger.

I walk nearer to the building and pause on the corner of 91st and Baltimore. Most of the front of the building is solid brick, coated with grime from the years of exposure to the South Chicago air. There are a few small windows on the second floor that I later learn look out of the company president's office. There is also a pair of glass doors leading into the plant. Next to the doors is a large truck loading bay. A truck is being loaded with cube shaped cardboard boxes by a Latino man, while a white truck driver stands on the bay looking lazily at nothing in particular. Next to the bay there are three cylindrical tanks. Each is about forty feet high and about ten feet in diameter. Parked next to the tanks is a large tanker truck. The white driver is sitting in the cab moving his head to unheard music. A black worker is attaching a hose between one of the tanks and the truck.

I cross the street and go to the doors. There is a small sign that says "Administrative Offices of the Chicago Shortening Corporation." I have arrived! I open the doors that go into a small hallway leading to a flight of stairs. The hall is air-conditioned and well lighted. Almost immediately the unpleasant odor disappears.

As I climb the stairs I feel calm. It will turn out to be the calm before a storm that will have a major impact on who I am today.

When I reach the top of the stairs, another door opens into a reception area. An attractive young white woman is at a desk. I can see several closed office doors.

"May I help you?"

"I'm here to apply for the maintenance job."

She smiles and hands me a clipboard with an application form attached and a pencil. She directs me to one of three chairs across from her desk. "When you're finished filling this out, I'll give it to the plant engineer. He should be back from lunch any minute, and he'll probably want to speak with you."

I fill out the form and hand it to her. As I do, a fifty-something white man in a brown sport jacket, white shirt, khaki pants, and penny loafers comes unsteadily through the same door I entered. He looks a bit disheveled; his thinning hair has been tossed by the South Chicago breezes. He looks at me.

"This gentleman is here about the job we advertised. Here is his application."

He walks over to where I am sitting and I stand. "I'm Bob Fulton, the plant engineer."

"I'm Dave Ranney." We shake hands.

"I'll have a look at this, and then I'll call for you. We may want you to take a short test."

This guy seems nice enough. But I note that he smells of alcohol. It is 2:00 in the afternoon. *Liquid lunch?* In a few minutes he comes out and motions me to his office. We both sit. "Tell me about yourself."

I tell him that my wife is an elementary school teacher whose family lives here in Chicago. We decided to move here to be closer to her family. I describe my last job in Cleveland, Ohio. I use the job at FAROC as a model for my tale, leaving out the part about centrifuges. I lie for about ten minutes straight. I am thinking: *This is getting easier all the time. I may be acquiring a new skill.*

He hands me a sheet with some questions. A few of them require knowledge of elementary algebra—simple for anyone with standard high school math. There are also some word problems that require basic reading comprehension and substantive knowledge, which I had gained from my brief stint in the centrifuge shop. It takes me about ten minutes. He is watching me the whole time. I hand him the sheet. He puts check marks in front of my answers; then he writes "100%" at the top. Feeling like a proud sixth grader, I smile a wide smile.

"Very good! Well, you have a job here if you want it. You'll start at $5.65 an hour. You will be in a union, Amalgamated Meat Cutters and Butcher Workmen. The contract specifies a month of probation. After that we can give you an increase." I nod and smile again. He puts out his hand. We shake. "Welcome to Chicago Shortening."

He takes me down the hall and introduces me to Maurie Green, who is vice president of the company. Maurie is a large man, about six feet tall and stocky. He is wearing a white shirt and a pair of dark slacks. We shake hands. His hands are rough. Bob then knocks carefully on the closed office door of Joe Cruse, the president. A smooth voice calls out, "Come in!" This is the office with the windows that look out onto 91st Street. Cruse is sitting behind his desk. I can see pictures on a bookshelf behind him. They show two children with a beautiful woman who looks like she could be a model. I assume she is his wife. Just as prominent are photos of three horses in a large green field. He rises, and Bob introduces me as the new maintenance man. We shake hands. His hands are cool, dry, and soft. He sees me staring at the photos. "Those are my horses. We have a horse farm in Kentucky." *It doesn't seem to occur to him that I might have been looking at his wife!*

I smile and nod but am otherwise silent. There is something about this guy that gives me the creeps. I look away from the pictures but can't meet his eyes. His manner is intimidating. Bob cuts in quickly: "Dave has good experience and scored a hundred percent on the test."

Cruse is wearing an expensive beige suit. His shoes are polished. His face and hands are tanned. Unlike Bob, he is neatly groomed—perfect haircut, not a hair out of place, and manicured nails. "You seem to be just the sort of fellow we need around here. *I am thinking "If only you knew I was a 'dangerous communist,'" as my former father-in-law once charged.* You and Bob and the other maintenance guys will keep things humming, I'm sure," he continued.

After we get back to Bob's office he whispers, "Be careful what you say to him. He's an asshole. Let's go and have a look around the plant."

We go out another door that leads directly into the plant. The heat and the smell nearly knock me over. I now identify the smell as what I experienced when opening up the centrifuge machines that came from the rendering plants. I can guess what the shortening in Chicago Shortening is made of. I remember a fellow worker at the last job joking about the liquid from the rendering process ending up in our cookies and fried chicken.

"So what do we make here?"

"Different kinds of cooking oils. We combine lard—the fat from pigs—and tallow—the fat from beef cattle—and process them in different ways for different customers. Some of our product goes to local restaurants. Other products are sold to large food processors. For example, Keebler Cookies is a major customer."

After a quick look around the plant, I make a mental note to scratch Keebler Cookies off the shopping list. There is a popular ad for the cookies on TV that shows the cookies being made by cute looking little cartoon elves. I guess I am now one of them.

"We get some of the lard and tallow from several local rendering plants. But most of it comes in on railroad tank cars from big producers like Iowa Beef Processors. There's a rail yard out back that I'll show ya. The raw materials are stored in those white tanks you may have noticed when ya came in."

We start to walk through the plant. I see a group of five black workers. They stare at me. They appear hostile; it may be my imagination. Bob doesn't introduce us. "Be careful walking here. The processing we do causes small amounts of product to escape into the air. It settles on the floor. We wash the floors all the time, but basically it's always slippery."

"Do we need masks?"

"You can wear one if ya want. I can get ya some." He gets out a pack of cigarettes and offers me one. We light up. He laughs waving the cigarette. "I never use masks myself."

We begin our tour. Tanks containing hot oil line the walls and hallways. They are hooked up to steam lines that go into coils at the bottom of the tanks that keep the material in the tanks very hot. The steam is constantly hissing as a special valve called a "steam trap" opens and closes if the steam begins to turn to water. The condensation from the traps sprays out into the air. There are also pumps attached to the tanks so that the processed shortening can be moved into rail cars or trucks.

We come into a room with a huge boiler that produces steam used to keep pipes and hoses clear and clean. A chemical additive is used to make it possible for water to be superheated before it turns to steam. I notice that there is steam and water squirting out a small leak that has opened up in the side of the boiler. I look at a pressure gage. It registers 250 pounds of pressure. "Err, isn't that a little dangerous? Couldn't this thing blow?"

"Naw, we're usin' the steam as fast as the pressure builds up. It never hits the max of three hundred. We have four boilers in the plant. One is off line bein' worked on, so we need the steam from this one to keep production up. We'll fix the leak when we get the other back on line. You can weld a patch on it next week."

"I don't know how to weld."

"I'll make sure the pipe fitters teach ya next week. It isn't that difficult."

We go into a separate room. A large red sign says, "Danger! Flammable Gas!" I see eight red gas cylinders that are marked "hydrogen." I drop my cigarette on the floor and grind it out carefully with my shoe.

"Yeah, good idea." He puts his out as well. "Some of what we make is hydrogenated oil. We combine hydrogen and oil under pressure. It's used by producers who want the product to stay hard, like M&M Candies. You know the ads that say 'melts in your mouth and not in your hand?' Well, we make that possible." *I make a mental note to scratch M&Ms off my shopping list as well.*

We go out the back door of the plant into the railroad yard. There are about eight large tanker rail cars on the tracks. A few are marked Iowa Beef Processors. Others have more obscure labels like GATX and ACFX. A number of workers, all black, are climbing on top of or under the cars, dragging hoses and attaching them to fittings.

Bob points to the workers. "Those are the pumpers. They take lard or tallow out of some of these cars and put finished product into others. Once a day an engine comes into the yard and brings cars in and pulls others out for shipment. The cars have steam coils in the bottom. The pumpers hook up steam lines to those cars so we can keep the oil hot enough until they move out."

A white guy in a flannel shirt holding a welding gun in his hand climbs out of one of the cars.

"I want ya to meet this guy. He's a pipe fitter who's on loan from the pipe fitters' union hall. There are two of 'em. We have a lot of pipe maintenance work. He's fixin' one of the steam coils I told you about. I'm gonna ask him to teach ya some of what he does so you can help 'em."

We walk over to the car. "Larry, this is Dave. We just hired him to work in maintenance. He doesn't know how to weld. I want ya to teach him some fundamentals so he can help you guys when needed."

Larry puts out his hand and we shake. He pulls off his welding hood, which had been tipped over the top of his head. He is in his thirties, blond with deep blue eyes. He stands about six feet tall, with a muscular build. I'd guess he weighs around two hundred pounds. He smiles. "Nice ta meet ya. Thank God you finally brought a white guy in, Bob. I was afraid you were gonna hire one of them niggers."

I feel myself stiffen. I try not to show my shock. I look to see if any of the workers nearby had heard. If they did, they don't react. Then I glance at Bob. He seems a bit embarrassed. "Well, he scored a hundred percent on the test!" Bob exclaims.

"Well, then, Dave, I'll be seeing ya. We'll teach ya a little welding for sure." He laughs and winks: "Glad ya passed Bob's test."

I'm feeling very unsettled and thinking to myself: maybe I shouldn't be here. But again, maybe there is something I can do. First Cruse and then pipe fitter Larry are glad to have a white man. Larry calls his fellow workers niggers. Let's see how that works out.

We go back into the plant. Bob shows me a huge machine. It's another cylindrical tank that is about the size of the ones I saw outside when I first came in. But this one is wrapped with heavy insulation and it's attached to an electrical panel covered with dials. A sleepy looking black worker is sitting at a table next to the dials. He is older than the pumpers—maybe in his fifties. He has a notebook and seems to be recording readings from the dials. He gets up and pushes some buttons on the panel. I hear a gurgling sound from inside the machine. He turns and smiles. Bob introduces us. "This is Jerome, and this is Dave our new maintenance guy."

Jerome smiles and puts out his hand. We shake. "I guess you aced Bob's test. I hear it was a bitch."

I feel embarrassed and probably look it. A blush is coming on. I shrug and smile, then look away. Bob explains the machine to me. "This is the deodorizer machine. It's the heart of the production process. All our tallow and lard is poured into the top of the machine, superheated, then Jerome here causes a vacuum to be drawn inside the machine, and the fatty acids that cause the bad odor are separated from the rest and thrown away."

Jerome turns and smiles as he opens and closes a few valves on the machine and throws a switch. We walk on. I see six Mexican workers pouring a thick white substance into blue plastic bags that are encased by a cube shaped cardboard box. They seal the bag and the box and load it onto a dolly. I recognize this as what I saw earlier going onto a truck in front of the plant. They are talking in Spanish as they work.

"This is our filling line. These are fifty-pound boxes of shortening that go mostly to local restaurants and fast-food establishments."

One shouts out: "Buenas tardes."

I reply: "Buenas tardes. Trabajaria in la mantenancia. Me llamo Dave"

They smile "Buena suerte, David"

I say to Bob, who seems to be surprised at this interaction, "My Spanish is very limited and basically shitty, but I can communicate a little."

"Good for you. That may come in handy."

We visit several more work stations and end up in the locker room. It is a grey dingy long narrow room with rows of lockers on each side. Beside the lockers are two rows of benches. There is a long wooden table that is in need of paint in the middle of the room. It is scarred with scratches and cigarette burns. It was grey at one time. The lockers were also grey but are now badly scratched. Some have been pried open. At the end of the locker room is a washroom with two sinks, two toilet stalls, two urinals, and a shower. The bathroom is in bad need of cleaning. In the locker room, the general odor of the plant is overcome by a mix of urine and marijuana smoke.

"This is where you can come and wash up. We have another room for the maintenance workers where you put your clothes and tools and take your breaks."

We walk across the hall to the maintenance workers' room. Bob gets out his keys and opens the locked door. I see an older white man in his sixties sitting in an easy chair. In addition to the chair, there is an old but respectable looking brown sofa in the large square room as well as six immaculate blue lockers and a newish looking card table. The man smiles and gets up. He is thin and stooped, with grey thinning hair. He is wearing a spotless white long cotton coat. He looks more like a TV doctor than a maintenance man in a shortening factory. There is a white hard hat sitting on the table.

"Frank, this is Dave Rainy, our new maintenance man. I'm goin' to ask him to accompany ya on the job this week so you can train 'im. Dave, this is Frank Pucinsky."

We shake hands. Bob walks into a second room connected to our special locker room. Frank and I follow. This room is lined with pumps, motors, and a variety of fittings, valves, and other machine parts on shelves. There is also a large shelf with special tools: a welding torch, nearby cylinders marked oxygen and acetylene, a set of welding tips, oversize pipe wrenches, an enormous screwdriver, and pry bars. In the middle of the floor is a workbench. There is a pump and a motor on the bench, both in the process of being rebuilt.

"When you're not on a specific job you can help Frank and the pipe fitters rebuild pumps and motors. These tools are for you guys to use. Be sure to put 'em away when you're done. If not, they'll get stolen. I assume you have your own tools. You can keep 'em in here and they'll be safe. You may have noticed that there's a time clock by the main door to the plant. Shift starts at 8:00 a.m. Sometimes you'll be asked ta work overtime or come onto other shifts. Your time card will be there tomorrow. After ya punch in you should come upstairs to my office and I'll give ya a key to these rooms. If I'm not in, I'll leave it with the girl at the front desk. Welcome aboard!"

We shake hands and he leaves. I turn to Frank. "So, I should meet you here in the morning?"

"Sure. You can learn a lot of stuff from me if you really want to. A lot of the knuckleheads in the plant want this job but don't wanna learn. I've worked in this place my whole life except for the time I was in the army. It used to be a meatpacking plant. I started processing bacon and other meats. Then I graduated ta maintenance. This was a Cudahy operation. But they consolidated and sold the building to Chicago Shortening. I stayed with the building. Been here forty years."

"You live near here?"

"Yeah, I walk to work. There've been a lot of changes to the neighborhood. But it's still a decent place to live."

"I just moved here, 93rd and Saginaw. Well, I'll see ya tomorrow."

"I'll walk out with ya." Frank puts on his white hard hat. I notice he walks with a decided limp. As we walk by the locker room I hear raucous laughter. The smell of marijuana is stronger. A handsome, muscular, dark-skinned black man in his twenties is walking toward the locker room door. He stops in front of us, smirking.

"Charles, this is Dave Rainy. He'll be working maintenance." This is Charles Sanders."

"Yeah, I heard. . . . Rainy? Is it raining?" He then begins a unique laughter routine. During the time I knew Charles, his laugh never failed to make me smile. He presses his lips tightly together, making his mouth look very small. Then the corners of his mouth turn slightly upward, his eyes squeeze shut, and his head begins to move up and down in rapid, short, jerky, silent bursts. The bursts evolve into body shaking, so violent that at first I think he might be having a seizure. Next, he releases a series of short bursts of air through his nose—gggh, gggh, gggh. Then suddenly his eyes and mouth fly open, and his head and upper body bend back and he explodes with a very loud *haw, haw, haw*!

I find myself laughing, and even Frank, whose demeanor is generally dour, is smiling.

"Actually, it's Ranney," I say while still laughing.

Charles has a puzzled look. "What?"

"My name. Its Dave Ranney, not Rainy."

Frank cuts in: "Oh, I'm sorry. I thought it was Rainy"

Charles is grinning ear to ear. "He ought to know his own name, Polacko; especially if he works maintenance. Okay then, Ranney it is." He is still smiling as he disappears into the locker room. A whiff of marijuana smoke escapes into the hall as he enters. I look at Frank who is back to his dour self.

"Reefer madness?" I laugh.

"These knuckleheads are always either bombed or stoned. Charles was both just now. Too bad. He and a few of the other guys are really smart. They could make somethin' of themselves."

"Management lets 'em get away with it?"

"Apparently. They don't exactly hide it, do they?"

Suddenly there is a loud voice coming from a speaker on the wall.

"*Frank Pucinsky, Frank Pucinsky, report to boiler number one!*"

Another black worker emerges giggling from the locker room. "Hurry up, Polacko. On the double!"

Frank looks at me and raises his eyebrows. "See ya tomorrow, Dave. Sorry I got your name wrong."

"No problem." We shake hands. Frank heads toward the far end of the plant, while I peel off to the nearest exit and leave.

★

In the next two weeks, Frank shows me the ropes. We change out motors, replace bearings, replace huge drums of chemicals that are used as additives to certain products and to waste water, replace steam and oil fittings for the hoses, unplug pipes that have become clogged with product, and repair pumps and motors. Some of the time I work with the two white pipe fitters who show me the basics of welding and how to weld lengths of pipe together. We take our breaks whenever we feel like it in our special (all white) locker room. I interact little with the other workers. I am especially uncomfortable taking lunch with the two pipe fitters, Larry and Ken. Both Frank and I are quiet as they talk on and on about "the niggers do this and the niggers do that," making fun of the "stupid shit they do," etc. They also talk about the "illegals" on the fill line . . . "lazy, don't speak English." I eat as fast as I can and leave with Frank.

"I'm glad you don't talk that way," I say.

"They haven't taken the time to know the other people here. I've worked with Bill and Henry for the last twenty years. We have a beer together now and then. The younger guys are another matter. I don't know what it is. Many of them are high all the time. That didn't used ta happen. I don't think it has anything to do with the colored. The guys my age were brought up differently."

"I'd like to get to know them. I might take my lunch in the locker room or down at the fill line from time to time."

"Well, good luck with that."

We get a call over the plant speaker system. It is Saul Hunter, a black foreman. He seems universally disliked. He tries to be a hard case and is actually a dumb shit who the front office can manipulate. "*Frank Pucinsky, Dave Rainy, report to the rail yard.*" I see Charles.

"Dave Rainy, is it raining?" He does his laugh thing. I find myself smiling and laughing at the joke that he now delivers several times a day. We see Saul. He points to a pipe just inside the door to the yard. "This pipe is blocked. The pumpers forgot to blow it out. The shit in there is packed with hydrogen oil." He then leaves.

Frank begins to grumble: "Forgot, my ass. They do this just to piss off the front office or Saul; same difference. We'll probably have to replace some pipe."

We try to heat the pipe with torches and push the blockage out with steam. It doesn't budge. We then find two places where we can open the pipe with wrenches. The section of pipe is solid with a white substance that feels like a piece of chalk.

Frank shakes his head. "If it does this in a piece of pipe, think what it does to your arteries if you eat it in cookies or crackers. Look for hydrogenated oil on the list of ingredients."

This is before the days when we are warned against eating hydrogenated oils. I register another item in my growing inventory of things to scratch off the shopping list. We wind up cutting off about thirty feet of pipe before we find the beginning of a clear line. We call the pipe fitters. They weld on a new section. Frank shows me how you can sometimes clear a line by running steam from the boiler through a special pump. "It won't work with the hydrogenated stuff."

★

I soon discover that the black workers all take lunch and breaks in the locker room. The Mexicans, most of whom work on the fill line, have fashioned some benches and sit near the line. The two groups don't mix. I try taking some breaks in both spots. The pipe fitters ask me why I do this. I tell them so I can get to know people. They shake their heads in disbelief. I suspect the new white maintenance guy is a bit of a disappointment to them.

The Mexicans speak mostly in Spanish. Mine isn't so good, but I understand enough to learn that they think the blacks are lazy drunkards and would steal the shirt off your back. The black workers have a similar low opinion of the Mexicans, or "Spanish" as they call them. They believe they are all "illegals," steal, and "they can't even speak American."

Initially my reception in both places is cool. But eventually they begin to get used to my strange habit of taking my breaks with them. I try to get a handle on issues in the plant. Workplace safety is one. There are a lot of minor accidents from falls and burns. Also, clothes and boots don't last long. Acid in the product and the chemicals used for cleaning or as additives eat boots away in no time. Work clothes soon become rags. The guys wash their own clothes in the plant by placing them in buckets filled with superheated water. There are always pants and shirts draped over the boilers or on makeshift clotheslines to dry. Many would like plant uniforms and a cleaning service. Everyone complains about the low pay and shitty benefits. There is a general consensus that the union is corrupt and worthless.

We belong to the Amalgamated Meat Cutters and Butcher Workmen Local 55. The union is the result of a 1950s merger of two large labor union federations—the AFL and the CIO. The meat cutters were part of the AFL and the Butcher Workmen were in the more radical CIO. I learn from Frank and other workers that Local 55 is a "consolidated local" and represents factories all over the metropolitan area. It has about seven thousand members. No one seems to know or care where the other factories are, who the other members are, when, where, or if there are membership meetings. The workers assume the union and Chicago Shortening are "mob connected."

When I sit down in the locker room Charles often tries to find a way to embarrass me. He will do or say something to make me blush and get everyone laughing at my expense. This is mostly done in a spirit of good fun, but it has a bit of an edge. Behind Charles's warm smile and infectious laugh there is anger and a certain coldness not only toward me but toward everyone. He often ridicules his openly gay brother James with homophobic taunts.

Slowly I get to know the others. Henry and Bill are the older workers who are friendly with Frank. The younger workers all tease them about their age—often with assertions about their declining sexual abilities. They are careful with Bill, however. He is a big and powerful man. While generally quiet and reserved, there is beneath the surface, not unlike Charles, a deep anger. When pushed too far he will stand up and menace his tormenters, and they back down quickly.

Then there is "Superfly," whose real name is Charlie Johnson. He is quiet and friendly and gets along well with everyone, including me. He does not seem to smoke dope and drinks very little during the day. He is of medium height and build with black skin. He does have a quirk that has earned him his nickname. He quits working about a half hour before punch-out time, goes to the locker room and takes a shower. Then he dresses in light beige slacks, a white shirt with a wide collar open at the neck, a brightly colored sport coat, a wide-brimmed white dress hat, and shined, spotless dress shoes. He resembles a movie character, a gangster called "Superfly" in a series of "blaxploitation" films that are popular with a lot of the black workers.

Willie is handsome, loud, and brags constantly about his sexual exploits. He routinely harasses any young or youngish woman who has the misfortune to walk by the plant while he is outside.

Oscears is known for his ability to move so slowly that at times he barely moves at all. And he talks as if he were mentally challenged. It is all an act. In reality he is among the most intelligent of all the workers and can, when need be, move with lightning speed. "When I was a kid," he once told me, "I grew up in the projects—Cabrini Green. Me and my boys formed a football team. We had full equipment that we got by raiding sports stores around the city. We would scout out a place, see where the football equipment was, and then pull a raid the next day. We just run in there, each grab what we need and run out so fast they don't have time to respond. We kept our equipment in an empty apartment at Cabrini. That was our locker room. We played kids from the other projects, but we also scrimmaged with the big city public school teams. Most of us could have been stars if we had stayed in school. We always won. I played running back."

The Mexicans on the fill line are tight, and my lack of language skills makes it difficult to get to know them very well. One of the older workers named José, who is bilingual, sometimes translates for me. Others are bilingual, and we talk in English. Mostly we talk about things related to maintenance. They tell me when the wheels on the dolly they use to move product to the loading dock need to be replaced. Or they point out a broken roller on a conveyer. Some of these workers are without papers and are afraid of the prospect of a raid by La Migra. None of them like the black workers.

Sometimes when I am needed to finish a job I stay over for the second shift. There is a clear leader in this group whose name is Lawrence. He works as a pumper, and everyone looks up to him. Lawrence is well over six feet tall. He has dark skin and wears black clothes, a beret, and dark glasses when he comes to work. Lawrence is articulate and political. He seems to have been touched by the Black Panthers, but I don't think he is a member.

One day Lawrence comes into work with a clipping from the *Chicago Defender*. It is a photo of one of the Sandinista revolutionaries in Nicaragua. The man in the photo is wearing camouflage battle fatigues, a beret, and is holding an automatic rifle. Lawrence pins the picture to the bulletin board in the locker room.

He smiles at me: "These fuckers have their shit together, don't they?" I nod in agreement, and the other workers crowd around to look at it. We have a discussion about Nicaragua and why they are having a revolution.

The second shift includes a Mexican maintenance man named Paulo. The black foreman and other supervisors called him Pablo. When we work together the call over the speakers comes: *"Pablo and Rainy, report to boiler number three!"* The supervisors treat Paulo like a child and speak to him painfully slowly and almost in baby talk. His English is generally better than theirs.

Then there is John Logan. He usually works third shift but sometimes comes in early when an extra pumper is needed. Like Frank, Henry, and Bill, he appears to be in his sixties. He is an alcoholic and is sometimes so drunk at the end of his shift that another worker punches out for him.

I come in early for my shift and find John dead drunk, passed out on one of the benches in the locker room. Two of us carry him to his car and put him in the passenger side. I drive the car to his house while the other worker follows. We get him inside and sit him on the couch and drive back. We have been spotted by Bob, the plant engineer who hired me. He is waiting when I get back. "Why do ya do that?"

"He needs the job, Bob."

"He'll kill himself one day. It's dangerous in there."

"Don't I know it."

"They'd fire you if you get caught."

"I won't if you don't tell." At 8:00 a.m. I take John's card and casually punch him out.

Bob himself is an alcoholic. He regularly goes across the street to a restaurant and bar called Sonny's and comes back bombed. He avoids the offices where Cruse and Green sit by coming into the back of the plant and going through a back door next to his office. I sometimes go in first to see if the coast is clear.

One of the most contradictory characters at Chicago Shortening is a second shift pumper. His name is Heinz. He is the only white pumper at the plant. He is short, stocky, in his forties, with long unruly gray hair. He arrives at work on a motorcycle when weather permits. He wears black leather—boots, pants, jacket, hat—and sunglasses. His leather jacket and motorcycle sport swastikas and patches that are replicas of the Confederate Flag. He carries a concealed pistol. He tells everyone he is a Nazi. Yet, unlike the pipe fitters, I never hear him say anything remotely racist. In fact, he is downright friendly with black and Mexican workers. His proclaimed Nazism gets to be sort of a joke. Some of the black workers give him the Nazi salute and shout "Sieg Heil" when they meet him in the hall. He returns the salute, smiles, and moves along. I'm not sure what this is all about.

There are a number of job classifications defined by pay differentials that are outlined in the union contract. At the bottom of the heap are thirteen cleaners. They work harder than anyone else. They have to constantly spray the floor with superheated water and various chemicals to keep the grease down. When there are spills caused by the pumpers, they have to clean it up. They are paid minimum wage. There are three loaders who make a bit more. They work out of a warehouse down the street where the trucks are stored and loaded with drums or cubes of product. Trucks bringing in other equipment are also unloaded there. There are seven workers on the filling line. This is the closest we have to an assembly line in the plant. They make a bit more than the loaders. Next are the pumpers—ten of them. Their job is to run hoses between tanks of finished product and the tanker trucks and railroad cars that take large quantities to buyers. Conversely, they also unload tallow and lard from trucks and railroad cars. There are nine machine operators, three on each shift. Jerome operates the deodorizer machine on first shift, but there is also a machine that feeds the line and another machine that removes solids from processed fat so that even in cool conditions it can always be poured and is perfectly clear. At the top of the heap are four maintenance men—Frank and me on first shift and one guy on each of the other two shifts. This does not count the two pipe fitters who are paid more than any of us through the pipe fitters' union. The company pays the union directly for their services, and they receive regular union wages through the union hall.

★

I meet one of the cleaners for the first time out in the rail yard. There has been a huge spill. The yard is covered with gravel, so cleaning up spilled shortening is a terrible job. I only know this worker by his street name,

Mr. Clean. He is named that not only because of his job classification as a cleaner, but because he could have been the model for the mascot used to sell the household cleaner of that name made by Procter & Gamble. Like the famous P&G icon, Mr. Clean is muscular. He has a perfect build and wears jeans and a tight white T-shirt that shows off bulging biceps and forearms and six-pack abs. He has very light brown skin and a shaved head. He is standing absolutely still in the middle of the mess in the rail yard staring at the sun with his eyes wide open! This alarms me. "Hey! Don't do that man. You can hurt yourself doing that."

He doesn't react. I can see Charles and Mayberry laughing. Charles shouts over in my direction, "Don't bother him, Dave. He's talking with his people."

Suddenly Mr. Clean snaps out of whatever trance he was in. He walks over to the building and pulls out a hose and shouts, "You guys get the fuck away. I'm lett'n' loose some superhot water."

If you got sprayed with superhot water, it could be lethal. Charles, Mayberry, and I clear out, and Mr. Clean lets loose with the hot stuff.

When we go into the building Charles explains that Mr. Clean had been a professional boxer and has taken a few too many punches. "But there's a guy you don't want to piss off," he laughs. "He now believes he's an alien stuck on this here earth."

"I think I know how he feels," I reply.

"Yeah, but his people, they live on the sun. He prays to them now and then. That's what he was doin'."

"Dave Rainy, Dave Rainy, report to boiler number one."

I go there and see Saul. He points to an area where there are about a dozen three hundred–gallon drums filled with a heavy chemical. "It's time to change out the drum at water treatment." He then walks away.

In the basement of the plant there is a small water treatment facility. The fatty acids from the deodorizer machine are mixed with boiling water and pumped into tanks. A chemical that causes the fatty acids to clump together and rise to the top is dripped into these tanks. A skimmer is perpetually moving on top of the material to push the smelly fatty stuff into drums for disposal. I don't know what they do with that stuff and don't ask. The process doesn't work very well in any case. I am told that residents of the neighborhood are always calling the city with complaints that their sewers are backed up because of the grease that is dumped into the city sewer system.

Once a month the drum dripping the chemical into the wastewater has to be replaced. I am given a special dolly that can be slipped under a full drum. Then by tilting the drum backwards I can wheel it across the floor and wrestle it into position. The drum is extremely heavy. I, on the other hand, am pretty small and weak. This task makes me feel downright puny.

With considerable effort I am able to get the edge of the dolly under the drum. But I am having trouble pulling it back so the dolly wheels are engaged. I am pulling with all my might, cursing, likely getting red in the face. The floor is slippery with accumulated oils. All of a sudden I lose my footing and go down hard. I feel a pair of strong hands grab hold of me and pull me to my feet. It is Mr. Clean. He smiles, looking every bit the part of the man on the household cleaner bottle.

"Hey don't do that man. You can hurt yourself doing that." He tosses my words of a few days ago back at me and does it with a huge smile. He then pulls the drum back with one hand and begins wheeling it to its destination with me tagging along behind him. He puts the drum in place.

"Thanks!"

"They shouldn't ask you to be doin' this. You is too small, Dave. Next time, come and get me. I can always help out."

He turns and starts to walk away, then stops and turns toward me. "Dave, something is goin' to happen soon, and I don't want ya ta be scared."

"What's that?"

"I'm goin' to disappear. My people is comin' soon and will take me home."

"The sun?"

"Yeah. A lot of these assholes think I'm crazy. But it's me who'll have the last laugh. You is always nice to me. Me and my people appreciate that. I wanted you to know."

"Thanks for the heads up and for telling me that."

He nods, never breaking his smile, and walks with purpose up the stairs to the main floor.

★

"Dave Ranney, Dave Ranney, please meet me at my office."

It's Bob. He has learned how to pronounce my name. We go to a place where there is a manhole that covers the sewer where the water from the plant enters the city sewer system. "There's another manhole on other side of this wall. That's where the city comes to test the water we're putting into their system. They're going to test it in about one hour. In a half hour I want you to turn off the valves that let our water into the system and put two hoses with fresh tap water into this manhole."

"What if they look on this side of the wall?"

Bob laughs. "They won't. They always stop at my office and have a few drinks before they do the testing. They just need ta take some clean water from the plant ta show their supervisor that they're testing regularly and the samples come out clean."

A half hour later, I'm standing next to the open manhole watching the water running from the hoses I have just put in. I hear the city inspectors on the other side of the wall talking as they remove the other manhole. I can hear Bob's voice. He is there as well. I would guess the city inspectors get more than a few drinks for their trouble. The water treatment is the minimum needed to avoid plugging up the whole sewer system. I see Bob later in the day. "Did we pass on our water discharge?" Bob laughs and gives me a friendly pat on the back.

I am having an easy but boring day. Not much of anything is happening in the plant. I go to the locker room to use the bathroom. Charles is sitting at the table drawing on a pad. I look over his shoulder. It is a perfect drawing of some familiar cartoon characters—Sylvester the cat and Tom and Jerry the mice. He isn't copying from anything. This is coming right out of his head. "You going for a job interview with Disney?"

Charles smiles. "You know what I like about Sylvester? It's when he says: 'I'm goin' to love those meeces to pieces.'" Then Charles starts with his unique laugh and soon all of the guys in the locker room are laughing too.

"That's really good. You have talent. Ever go to art school?"

"Naw. I can draw, but what good will it do me here?"

"You don't have to stay here forever. If you do you'll end up looking like Polacko."

He makes a face: "I turn white? Shiiit!" More laughing.

Things get quiet and Charles looks me in the eye. "Dave?"

Mayberry lights up a joint and passes it to Charles. He takes a hit and tries to pass it to me. I shake my head no and he passes it to James.

"Dave?"

I'm beginning to feel uncomfortable. "What?"

"Do you think you're a nigger?" He is looking directly at me. He has a smirk on his face. Everyone else is looking at me too. I feel an enormous uncontrollable blush coming on. "Come on man, I'm serious! Do you think that you're a nigger?"

I don't know what to say or do. So I sigh and get to my feet and start for the door. I shake my head and mumble to myself: "I, I don't know—wh"

Before I can finish the sentence Charles breaks in. He speaks very slowly emphasizing every word.

"Dave . . . don't . . . know . . . if . . . he's . . . a . . . nigger."

Everyone is looking at me now to see how I'll react. I feel like bolting for the door of the locker room. But Charles suddenly begins his laugh routine, and before he is through everyone in the room is laughing, including me. I sit back down. Charles gets up and slaps me on the back and walks out of the locker room.

Things are beginning to get routine. I am getting better at welding and can do all the basic jobs. I work on my own unless I am doing something that requires two men. Bob sends me to night school to take a course in electricity. I learn the basics so I can do some of the electrical work and understand better how electricity works. The initial hostility from the black workers is pretty much gone now. The black workers continue to talk negatively about the Mexican workers being illegal. I bring a bunch of the pamphlets we produced at the Workers' Rights Center titled "Since When Has Working Been a Crime?" I talk about the Fugitive Slave Laws that made their ancestors "illegals." I leave some of the pamphlets in the locker room, not sure if this has any impact or not.

When I come in for lunch Charles is holding forth. "We're talking about what the best movie ever made was, Dave."

"What did you decide?"

"I'm just getting to that." Charles takes a pint bottle of a cheap wine out of his locker, unscrews the cap, takes a long drink before opening a package of Wyler's powdered lemonade mix, and pouring it into the bottle. The cap is replaced and he shakes the mixture vigorously. The workers called it "shake 'n bake." He pushes it in my direction. "Want some?"

I shake my head.

"Awe, you're no fun Dave. No reefer, no shake 'n bake. What do you do for fun?"

I deliberately don't react.

"Okay. The best movie ever made is *Orca the Killer Whale*." He emphasizes the word killer and looks directly at me. "Here's why. Orca was the baddest dude that ever lived. He always swam the oceans with his lady at his side. They'd swim real deep and fuck for a while. And after they cum, they'd jump clear out of the water, swishing their big black asses in the sunlight. But one day some honkies come in a boat and snatch Orca's lady. They shoots her with a tranquilizer gun, haul her ass right up on their boat. See, they fixin' to put Orca's lady in a zoo. Well, Orca's lady is carryin' his babies, and when they bring her onto the boat she loses the babies and dies herself so none of them will have to live in a fucking zoo. But what the honkies don't figure is just how bad Orca really is, and that by now he is one angry motherfucker. For a while he just cools it so the honkies will think everything is okay. But then all of a sudden he puts it to 'em—swims into the harbor pulling down fuel lines and setting houses on fire. In the end he gets the dude who killed his lady out on this big sheet of ice and tips the ice up so the guy slides screamin' right into Orca's mouth. He eats 'im!"

Charles is looking serious now and looking me in the eye. I know something else is coming. "So, Dave, what do you think is the greatest movie ever made?" Charles is testing and teasing me again. I have come to like Charles, especially when he isn't high on something, but I remain aware of the intensity about him that is very angry, perhaps dangerous.

I am silent as Charles and I have a brief stare down. The locker room is silent as a joint and a bottle of shake 'n bake make the rounds.

"My vote would be for *Moby Dick*."

Charles responds. There is a bit of a twinkle in his eye. "Whose dick?"

"Moby Dick. It's the name of a book and a movie. Moby Dick is a whale. He's bigger and badder than Orca. If he and Orca ever met up he would swallow Orca like he was a minnow. Also, Moby is white. He's killed a lot of people."

The locker room is even quieter. Charles has lost the twinkle and is staring at me intently.

I continue: "Most of them, honkies."

I smile at Charles. Then his head begins to move and lips pucker. There is the nose sound, "gha, gha, gha. Charles jumps to his feet bends back and lets out with the "*haw, haw, haw!*" Everyone is laughing. Charles walks up to me and hits me on the bicep with his fist. It is playful but it stings.

★

I've been at Chicago Shortening for a little over a year now. I feel at home there as much as anywhere except for the Workers' Rights Center. Beth is working as a secretary at the Erikson Institute, a graduate school in child development located near South Chicago in the Hyde Park community. Things seem strained between us. She is depressed a lot. But she is active in many of our political activities. When my son Chris comes to visit she is particularly unhappy. She tells me she is not cut out to be a mother. I silently tend to agree.

There are things going on at the Center. A group of Mexican women have asked for help. They work at a factory called Gateway Industries that is located nearby. Gateway makes auto seat belts and a dishwashing soap. That combination: go figure. The company announces they are closing the plant and moving to Mexico. The women workers have already been treated poorly, make minimum wage, and have few benefits. They are not organized by a union but decide they want to picket the plant to protest the move. Kingsley and two other STO members pitch in to provide support. I help out when I'm not at work.

They decide to try to initiate a boycott of one of the company's products, Pink Lady dishwashing soap. I paste up boycott posters around the neighborhood and pass out flyers at the steel mill gates and, of course, at Chicago Shortening.

Kingsley invites representatives of management to meet at the Workers' Rights Center. When they arrive the women workers are hiding in an alley but crowd in once they're inside, blocking their exit. After a sometimes heated discussion, an agreement is drafted with the company promising to hire the women at their Michigan facility, about an hour's drive from South Chicago, as positions open up. The women don't want to go along with the plan, because it involves jobs that may never materialize. One of the women takes the agreement and tears it up.

★

It is a slow day at work. I'm in the maintenance workroom rebuilding a worn-out pump when I a get a call. *Dave Ranney, Dave Ranney, please report to Mr. Green's office.* The call is from one of the secretaries this time. I walk past the locker room door as Mayberry comes out. "A date with Lisa! Let us know how she is. I may try her myself."

When I get to the office Maurie tells me to replace a burned-out bulb in the florescent light on the ceiling above his desk. I move the desk out of the way and leave to get replacement bulbs and a stepladder. When I come back Maurie is standing outside his office talking to Lisa, the secretary. I also notice two men in dark suits coming up the stairs from the street. I replace the bulb and am carrying the old bulbs and stepladder back to the shop floor as one of the men is showing Maurie some identification. I glance at the open wallet as I walk by and see a badge. They are from Immigration and Naturalization—La Migra!

I hurry down to the fill line and glance out a door to the street. I see a van and several other men in suits around the plant. I shout to the fill line workers, "La Migra estan aqui!"

Without a word they move out a back door into the railroad yard and hopefully melt into the neighborhood. Two pumpers see them go and walk over to the fill line. I begin to seal up accumulated boxes of product and stack them on a dolly. It is ten minutes before normal break time. Oscears asks, "What's goin' down, Dave?"

"Immigration is here. Some of them could be shipped back to Mexico. They could lose their wives and kids. Give me a hand, okay?" Oscears and Chico pitch in. Then Maurie with the two Migra agents approach the line.

Maurie: "Where the hell is everybody?"

"They told me they needed to take an early break and asked us if we would help out until regular break time."

Maurie turns to the two agents. "Someone tipped them off, I guess." The agents and Maurie leave. I doubt Maurie wanted the raid—too much trouble for the company. He knows I tipped them but never says anything to me about it.

The bell for break rings and the three of us go to the locker room. Oscears tells the other guys about it. They all laugh. There is no discussion of the merits of our action. I decide to let it go at that but thank Oscears and Chico. After the break I walk back to the line. All but one of the workers are back.

"Gracias David."

"You sure they're gone? There was a van and some other agents outside."

"Yeah. And we have some people watching."

★

There are a lot of days at the Shortening when there is little to do, and I spend the day walking around talking to fellow workers about this and that. But today is different. *"Dave Rainy, go here!"* *"Frank Pucinsky, go there!"* Then *"Dave Rainy, go somewhere else."* Etc., etc. Frank and I are running all over the place. I am told to unplug one of the pipes. This one does not have hydrogenated oil in it so it can be cleared by heating the oil or the pipe. The preferred method is to run steam through a pump that pushes the steam under pressure into the pipe. Then you turn the steam and the pump off and try to blow out the pipe with compressed air. Often you repeat the process several times. I pull the cast iron cap off the pump and peer in. The hardened oil has not reached as far as the pump. I put the cap back on with a pipe wrench and turn on both the steam and the pump. Then: *"Dave Rainy, Dave Rainy, Frank Pucinsky, Frank Pucinsky, go to the motor at boiler one!"*

This motor runs a pump that is central to the entire production process. I go there on the double. Frank is already there. The motor has burned out. It is a big motor and pump and takes two of us to change it out. Saul the foreman is standing there with his hands in his pockets.

"Change out this motor!" Saul barks.

"Brilliant, Saul," Frank shouts back.

We pull the whole thing apart, and I go to the maintenance shop to get another motor. We get everything up and running in less than an hour. I then return to the line blockage problem. Forgetting I had put the pump and line under steam pressure, I put my pipe wrench on the pump cap and begin to loosen it. Suddenly there is an explosion. I feel the iron cap clip my ear as it blows off, (eventually ending up embedded in the ceiling). Worse yet, I get hit directly in the face by the superhot oily steam so hard that it knocks me down. My face first feels like it is on fire, then it turns numb. I am on my hands and knees but am blinded. Everything is a blur. I instinctively crawl to a nearby sink and pull myself up. I turn on the cold water and frantically splash water on my face. Eventually I stick my whole head under the running water and turn my face toward the faucet. Saul comes up behind me and tries to pull me away from the sink.

"What the fuck are you doin', Rainy?!"

"Let me go. I know what I'm doing." Saul lets go and steps back. Other workers are gathered around. I am feeling woozy and still am unable to see.

Saul: "Tell me what happened. Why'd you pull the cap off the pump with a full head of steam."

Me: "Shut the fuck up and get me to a hospital." A bunch of workers half carry me up the stairs and sit me on a bench near a loading dock. I can feel the cool air on my face. It is a bit of a relief. Someone sits next to me and begins to speak. I recognize Bob's voice.

"Dave, I'm going to have to make a report. Tell me exactly what happened."

"Visit me in the hospital, and I'll tell you all about it."

"Yeah, you're right. You've got skin hangin' off your face."

"I'm glad ya told me that. For Christ sake, get me to the hospital."

"Saul! Get your car and take Dave to emergency at South Chicago Community."

Saul pulls his car into a loading dock and a bunch of people load me into his car. He lurches forward with tires squealing. After a few minutes the car stops.

"We're there already?"

"No. I'm lost. I guess I don't know where the hospital is. Thought I did."

"Shit, Saul! What street are we on?" I still can't see.

"Don't know. I don't live in this neighborhood."

"Go to the next intersection, stop and tell me what street we are on and what the cross street is." I am in real pain now and talking through gritted teeth.

"Take it easy, Dave. We'll find it."

I mutter something like: "Great! A blind burned white boy and a knucklehead." Saul does as I suggest and I am able to guide him to the hospital.

"I see it!" He speeds forward and comes to an abrupt halt. There is a commotion outside the car. The door opens and people are helping me out and easing me onto a gurney. A woman's voice: "Chicago Shortening called. What took you guys so long?"

Me: "It's a long story! I'm blinded and having a lot of pain. Feels like my face is on fire." Someone places a cloth over my eyes. I feel movement. People are running with the gurney into and through the hospital. Just like the TV doctor shows. We stop. I feel people cutting away my clothes, removing my boots and socks. The cloth is taken briefly from my eyes. I am aware of light. It hurts. Everything hurts from my neck up.

"This will make you more comfortable." I feel the prick of a needle in my arm, while someone else is sticking another needle in the other arm. I awake in a cool but comfortable room. I am in a bed. I instinctively put my hands to my face. It is covered with bandages.

I shout: "What about my eyes? Am I blind?" I am in a state of panic. I feel a hand on my shoulder.

"It's Kingsley, Dave. Beth will be over soon. I asked about your eyes. They think they may be all right. I hear you ran cold water into your eyes and over your face. Lucky you did that. But they won't know for sure about any of it for a few days." Someone from the Shortening plant had called Beth, and she had called Kingsley.

★

I share a room with an older black man who is dying of cancer. I can hear people around his bed praying. A woman puts a hand on my shoulder. She is part of the prayer circle but has come over to my bed. "You've had a bad accident, honey. Can you see?"

"Not yet. But they think I'll be okay. Thanks for asking."

"We're from African Baptist Church, right near your factory. We are prayin' for our brother. We can have a prayer circle around your bed too."

"Thanks anyway, but I'll get the prayers from where you're standing if you don't mind. Besides, it sounds like he needs them much more than I do. I hear he has the cancer. Hope he'll be okay."

"Thanks honey. We'll pray for you too." She goes back to her circle.

A few days later the bandages are removed. I can see, although everything is still a little blurry. I get a nurse to help me stand and try to use the bathroom on my own. Success! When I'm in there I look in the mirror for the first time. I am shocked by my own image. My face is covered with one big scab. I look like an uncooked meatball!

★

My roommate dies one day. I see the nurses take him away, followed by the Baptist prayer group. The kind woman who had come over to my bed is crying. She turns my way as she leaves the room. I nod at her. She nods back and gives me a weak smile. Then she is gone too. The man is soon replaced with another man in dire condition. I guess I am in a "dire condition" room at the hospital. I can't remember how long I am there. I have a steady stream of visitors from the Workers' Rights Center and some of my leftie friends. A number of workers from Chicago Shortening bring a bottle of shake 'n bake in a paper bag and offer me a swig. I decline. Bob shows up and gets his report. He tells me he is glad I am better. Saul never visits. Maybe he got lost on his way back and will never be seen again!

★

When I am able to return to work I am told to be careful. The main concern from management seems to be that I not file a disability claim through Workers' Comp that will impact their taxes. I don't. I'm sore but not really disabled. Workers' Comp does cover my hospital and doctor bills and a portion of lost wages. That is automatic.

For a few months I wear sunglasses all the time. I am very careful around pumps. At first I hang out more in the maintenance locker room and talk to Frank and the two pipe fitters because I can lie down on the sofa. One day the pipe fitters begin their routine: "stupid niggers this and stupid niggers that." I tell them I hate this kind of talk and that the people they are talking about have become friends of mine. They soon leave the room and go back to work. Frank remains.

"I don't like that talk either. They don't really know anything about people. They have never really had a conversation with a colored guy. So what do they know? Believe it or not, the prejudice around here used to be worse. Did I ever tell you how I met Bill and Henry?"

"No."

"When I turned seventeen the depression was on. I couldn't find work. I had dropped out of school to look for work and found a few odd jobs. My family needed the money bad. My dad was a friend of the alderman and one day I was playing ball at the park and the alderman shows up and motions me to come over."

"He whispers: 'There's a job open at Cudahy packing plant on 91st and Baltimore. I put in a word for ya. Get over there on the double. If someone else gets there first they'll probably give the job to them.' I had to take a leak but I didn't stop to do that. In fact, I left my ball glove and bat on the field and started to run. I showed up out of breath, found a foreman and was told to start working immediately. I still had to take a piss. But I had to first work on the packing line until the break was called. By the time we got a break I had pissed my pants. I was embarrassed. I followed two colored guys into the locker room. I was beet red. One of them went to his locker, got a clean pair of pants. He handed them to me. That was

Henry. The other laughed and said: 'Don't worry about it. That's what pants are for.' That was Bill. We've been friends ever since."

"There was another white guy on the job that everyone—colored and white—liked a lot. His name was Tom. One day we were on the line and he just fell over dead. Heart attack! They took him to a funeral home for the wake. I knew the guy who owned the place. He was a buddy of my dad's. Another Pollack. A bunch of us went over from work. As we walked in the owner says, 'We don't allow niggers in here.' He turns to Henry, Bill, and a few other colored guys. 'You guys get out or I'll call the cops.'

"'Look Stan,' I says, 'We're all friends of Tom. We're here to pay our respects.

"'You know better than this, Frank. You and the other white guys will have to stand in for the niggers. They're not comin' in here.'

"'I turn to Bill, Henry, and the other colored guys. I am embarrassed and angry. There are about six other white guys. They're pissed too. I say to Bill and Henry. 'Do colored funeral guys let white folks into their funeral homes?'

"Bill answers, 'I reckon they would. I'm not sure.'

"I says, 'Call one and find out.'

"Bill goes out and comes back about fifteen minutes later. Stan is by this time sputtering mad. 'I mean it Frank. They'll have ta' get out.'

"Bill says, 'They says that if they bury a person, all the friends and family are welcome.'

"I push past Stan. Tom's wife is standing by the casket, dressed in black and cryin'. I talk to her and explain what's going on. She tells Stan to let us in. He is adamant. She gets angry and says. 'Then we'll bury Tom at the other place.' All the guys push into the room. We close the casket and carry it outside as Stan screams. We put the coffin in the bed of Bill's pick up. And the wake moves to the colored funeral home."

I am staring at Frank, spellbound. But suddenly I get a call: "*Dave Rainy, Dave Rainy, report to the rail yard.*" I give Frank a friendly pat on the back and make my way to the yard. A car needs a new steam fitting. I am about to go back to the shop to get the new fitting, when I hear a scream. I look around and spot Charles on the top of one of the tanker cars. His hand is caught under the heavy lid.

Pumpers, when moving product into tanker rail cars lift heavy three-inch hoses onto the top of the car. They stick the end of the hose into the car through a hole in the top and tie the hose securely into place with twine. After the pumping is finished, they blow the line out with steam. Then they cut the hose loose and let it fall to the ground and close the heavy steel lid. Charles had apparently cut the hose loose but lost his grip on the heavy top and slammed it on his hand. A number of us race to the car, lift the lid, and help Charles down the ladder. His hand is brutally crushed. He is in great pain but the tears in his eyes are about something else.

"This is my drawing hand, man," he says to me. "I'll never draw again."

His dreams are crushed as badly as his hand. I sharply remember my own fears about my eyes after my accident. *What would have happened to me—my ability to read and write—if I had been blinded?* Saul is directed to take him to the hospital. I wonder if he can remember how to get there?

A few weeks after Charles's accident, one of the union business representatives makes a rare appearance in the locker room during the shift change. Workers from both shifts are getting ready to go home or to start work. The union rep is a short, skinny weasel of a man in a maroon sport coat, beige slacks, and white shoes. He has a whiny, high-pitched voice. His name is Jack. He enters the locker room and stands up on a bench.

"Hi guys."

The workers mock him in unison and falsetto voices: "Hi guys!"

Jack turns a little red in the face. I can see sweat on his forehead. "I'm your union representative."

"Big fucking deal!" someone shouts. "You want to pay my hospital bills?" The workers are laughing with contempt. Everyone starts talking at once with complaints about hospital bills, low pay, and the dues check off. When things quiet down he continues.

"You need to choose a negotiating committee and pass these suggestions on to them." Suddenly the room is quiet and sullen. Some open their lockers and begin to change into their street clothes or their work clothes. They are openly rude to the union man, slamming locker doors and turning their backs while he is talking. "Your union has decided to take advantage of the contract provision of a wage reopener this year and negotiate a better contract. We want to know what you would like to see happen." The second shift pumper, Lawrence, steps forward.

"Put us on the negotiating committee!" It is a declaration, not a question.

"Frank is already representing you. But you can choose one of your own and the Mexicans can too."

"Frank don't represent us. And the Mexicans will choose José. He's a sellout."

"You can also talk directly to me if you want. But I'm sure Frank will pass your suggestions on in the negotiations."

"For starters, we want the vote to be held here. No bullshit mail-in vote like last time. And we want some of us in this room to be present when the votes are counted."

"Well, we can talk about that. Good suggestion." Anyone else?" No one else speaks up. Jack gets down off the bench, bids us a good evening, and leaves in a hurry.

"What bullshit," Lawrence says. Everyone nods in agreement.

James answers, "The good thing is that that's the last we'll probably see of him for another three years at least. The rep we had last time, Mason, he was worse than this guy. I wonder if he still works for the union?"

I ask what's going on. The workers seem completely of one mind about the union, nodding in agreement as Lawrence explains. "Two years ago the union and company signed a contract. It was supposed to last for three years. Not sure why they're openin' it now. It was shit in any case. The company pays off the union just like they pay off everyone else. Get this. They sent us ballots in the mail. We had to mail them to the union hall. No one voted for it, but they said it passed." Everyone in the room nods and murmurs agreement. "Frank has been our union steward since Local 55 came in. I don't know who chose him. We never voted for him. In fact, I don't know how Local 55 got in here."

"Frank's not so bad a guy," I say.

"Hmm," Lawrence grunted. "He's always part of negotiations. I don't trust him or José. You know what I think? The union and the company is both part of the mafia. This whole shortening thing is a front to launder mafia money and the union is paid off to keep it lookin' legit."

★

My son, Chris, who is ten years old, has come to spend the rest of the summer with Beth and me. I have enrolled him in a day camp run by the YMCA across the street from Chicago Shortening. I bring him to work with me. But the Y doesn't open until 9:00; I punch in at 8:00. I sit him on a step at the front of the plant and tell him to wait while I make a few rounds to see that everything is okay in the factory. Then I come back to sit with him. He peers into a dark entrance of the plant.

"Dad, can I go in there?"

"It's kinda nasty and scary."

"I want to."

"Okay." I take him into the plant. We walk down a narrow aisle lined with hot tanks all hissing steam. The foul odor gets worse. The floor is slippery. The passageway is dimly lit and the steam in the aisle makes it even more difficult to see. I hold his hand and stay between him and the tanks. Suddenly, Chris jerks at my hand and stops. "Dad! I changed my mind. Can we go back?"

"Sure." We go back. I take him over to the Y when it opens. They will keep him there until my shift ends. He never asks to go into the plant again.

One day Bob comes into the maintenance shop. He tells Frank and I to shut down one of the boilers to let it cool. He explains that one of the boiler inspectors will be by. We will need to cool the boiler enough to open the door so he can look inside of it. We do this and are standing by the boiler with the door open. The inspector has been upstairs with Bob in his office for about an hour. We can see Bob and the inspector walking unsteadily toward us. They are laughing about something. The inspector pulls out a flashlight and shines it in the general direction of the boiler. He never looks in our direction but keeps walking with Bob. "Looks good boys," he calls over his shoulder. "You can button it up now." He and Bob keep walking toward the stairs that will take him out of the plant.

The deodorizer machine keeps breaking down. It won't hold a vacuum long enough for the separation of the fatty acids that cause the odor. This stops the production process in the entire plant. Each time this happens, Jerome shuts the machine down and inspects the insulation to see if there are any leaks in the wall of the chamber. When he finds one he cuts the insulation away from the spot and locates what is always a small pinhole—enough to cause the breakdown. The pipe fitters weld patches over the pinhole and replace the insulation.

It is happening with enough frequency that Bob wants to find out what is going on. He gives me a small gadget. He explains that when I push a button while holding it against the wall of the deodorizer tank it sends a sonar signal through the wall and measures the wall's thickness at this point. Bob asks me to cut a series of holes in the insulation and sample the wall thickness. I take about a dozen measurements, and make a map of the deodorizer wall to show where each sample was taken from. I bring it to Bob. "How thick are the walls supposed to be?" I ask.

"A half inch."

"Well this thing is shot. Some places the walls are less than one-sixteenth. I'd say it's time to buy a new deodorizer."

Bob laughs. "That'll never happen. We now have an idea where it's the most worn. This will help locate the leaks when they occur."

"If it gets so thin and doesn't break through in pinholes, couldn't the whole thing implode, kill Jerome, maybe me?"

"That's pretty far-fetched, Dave."

"But not impossible." He waves me away. There is no real investment going on in the plant. There are holes opening up in the boilers and tanks, now the deodorizer. Last week the U.S. Department of Agriculture closed the plant for a day. We had to do some special cleaning and patch up a number of tanks that might impact the quality of the "edible oils," as they call what we make. We are always instructed to do the minimum. The place is beat to shit. Maybe the guys are right about this being primarily a laundry for mafia money.

Negotiations on the new contract begin. The black workers select James to represent them. He is very reluctant and nervous about it. But none of the others want to do it. Lawrence and Charles tell me that because the process is a farce no one wants to take the blame for the results. So Charles makes his brother James volunteer. Heinz volunteers as well—to represent the "Aryans" I suppose. The Mexicans, as expected, select José. As union steward, Frank is "ex officio."

Frank tells me that at the first negotiating session Jack brought in a preprinted list of "demands." None of the negotiating committee members representing the workers had seen the "demands" before negotiations started. They are upset. James quits immediately, saying the whole thing "gives me a headache." The company appoints Henry to take his place.

The guys in the locker room seem to have given up at this point. But they are angry. The following day, after talking this over with Kingsley,

I post a signed letter in both English and Spanish on the bulletin board. Having talked to workers over the past two weeks I compile a list of demands for contract negotiations. My letter lists these and encourages everyone to force our negotiating committee to take them to the next negotiating session. I also raise the possibility that if this does not work we can take steps to decertify Local 55 and work together to find a union that will represent us. My letter is well received.

At the next negotiating meeting, Heinz presents counterdemands based on my letter. The company and union both balk and negotiations are halted. Following that meeting, the company begins to harass workers for rule violations. It is announced that all workers must punch in and out in their work clothes, depriving them of a petty informal privilege of having clean up time as part of work time. Superfly is particularly pissed off about this, but other workers object as well. The company begins to issue warnings for taking informal breaks and states that people who drink or take drugs on the job will be fired. The guys seem to agree that all this is intended to send a message that things could go worse for them if they continue to resist the negotiations process.

About a week later I see a union business agent James Mason in the administrative offices. He enters Cruse's office and they have a closed-door meeting that lasts about an hour. He then meets separately with Frank and Henry. Frank tells me that Mason tried to discredit me and Heinz—said we are troublemakers. And he advised them to avoid any contact with us.

There are two more negotiating meetings that go nowhere. Heinz is adamant about the worker's demands, and he claims that Frank, Henry, and José just sit there silently. On June 1, the company makes its "final offer." The meeting breaks down without agreement, and Heinz goes to work on his shift. The contract expires on June 3, after which a strike could be authorized. After Heinz leaves, Jack, representing the union, takes Frank, Henry, and José out for coffee. He gets them to agree to extend the contract "a few days." The following day, he and Mason come to the plant and go to Cruse's office. There they sign a two-week extension of the present contract, eliminating the possibility of a legal strike during this period.

Heinz is furious when he finds out. He circulates a petition calling for a walkout at midnight on June 3. He brings it to me. I am working four to midnight that day, so I will be coming off my shift when his strike is supposed to start. He shoves it in my face. "Here sign this."

"This isn't goin' to work, Heinz."

"Just as I thought. You don't have the balls for it. You're in league with Frank."

"No, I'll be there, but you can't be successful by trying to bully people into it."

"Are you with us or against us?" he shouts into my face.

"See you at midnight, Heinz. Hope I'm wrong." He continues to sputter as I walk away.

We are supposed to meet to start the strike in the rail yard. At 11:00 I get a call on the speakers. *"Dave Ruiny, Dave Rainy, come to the loading dock."*

I go. I see Maurie and the shift foreman standing on the dock. There is a police car pulled into the loading area. I look out and see other patrol cars and a few cops in suits standing around. Maurie walks up to me. "We're goin' to shut down and lock up. You go around and make sure all the entrances are locked and secure. Then tell your buddies that if anyone fucks with the trucks or any equipment it will mean serious prison time." I am accompanied by the foreman as I lock up.

"Are you guys really going to strike?"

"You'll know soon enough," I answer

When we finish I go to the clock and punch out and then head out to the rail yard. Heinz is there with only two other workers. The strike is broken before it starts.

Two days later, first and third shift workers are called to assemble at the filling line at shift change time. Cruse and Green are there representing the company. Mason and Jack speak for the union. Mason briefly explains the terms of the company offer. No written version is available nor are his remarks translated into Spanish. Each of us is given a small piece of paper with Yes and Si printed on one half and No on the other. We are handed pencils and told to mark the ballot. They have a wooden box with a slot on the top that is locked with a padlock. We put our marked ballot in the box and are asked to return the pencils.

Oscears shouts, "What about the second shift workers? Will their votes count?"

Green responds, "They will vote at the beginning of the shift."

"I'll keep the ballot box in my locker until that vote is taken," Oscears replies. He moves to take the box but is restrained by one of the shift foremen. Cruse, Green, and our two union representatives give a hardy laugh.

Cruse: "We are putting the ballot box in a locked room. Let's give this man light duty today so he can keep an eye on the room and make sure no one enters." Everyone is sent back to work. But at 10:00 a.m. the first shift workers are summoned once again to the fill line. Cruise and Green are there grim-faced. Our equally grim-faced union representatives, Jack and Mason, are at their side. A Latina secretary is also with them. Cruse speaks, and as he does the secretary translates.

"I want you to know that last night I received an anonymous call. I wasn't going to say anything, but my family and our attorney have asked me to do so. The caller stated that if the workers don't get a better deal on the contract, the plant will be bombed." Nearly all the workers start to laugh. Mason steps forward. "This is serious!" he shouts. "I am telling all of youse that this sort of shit will not be tolerated by the union."

We are then dismissed, with several of the workers still chuckling over the stupidity of the ruse. But later we realize that for the past half hour the storage room with the ballot box had been unwatched. Oscears had arranged with other workers to guard the room if he got called away. But everyone was required at the "bomb scare" meeting. When the next shift comes in, they are called to the filling line to vote. Heinz is given a key to the room and goes to get the box. When he gets back he says it is not where Oscears said it would be and that he can't find it. They send a second shift foreman to the locked room, and he comes right back with the box. The vote is then taken and the votes counted immediately in front of the workers. The result: twenty-six yes, sixteen no.

Heinz and Lawrence conduct an informal "exit poll" over the next three shifts. No one admits to voting for the contract. Then Heinz, Lawrence, and I circulate a petition calling for a revote on the contract. Forty-four workers sign.

While Cruse is out of the plant, Mason and Green sign the new contract. They are in such a hurry that they don't even wait for Joe Cruse, the company president. When the workers find out, Lawrence puts his own notice on the bulletin board. It is handwritten. He does not sign his name, but everyone knows it is his. It reads:

June 6, 1978

This is an appeal to all employees of Chicago Shortening Corp.

As you all know we were shafted by the union. On June 5, 78, we were gather together to vote on the acceptance or rejection of the Co. 3yrs. contract. Your so call union official fail to interpret the contract completely. The voting procedure was most definitely a fraud. To my knowledge the meeting was supposed to take place on June 6, 1978. Your union steward fail to advise us, (the employees) for reasons that I will not reveal at this time.

The use of psychology is most definitely in full play among our superiors toward us, but there are still a few of us who have the knowledge of its use.

I make a plead to you to stand up for what you know is right. It's time to challenge these imperialistic minded higher ups and put an end to this childish game.

Any question regarding the above said information will be answered.

★

The afternoon after Lawrence's letter, workers get together between first and second shift and decide to hold a formal meeting with all three shifts the following day. Despite some harassment from the foremen, thirty-nine workers attend. We have someone to translate into both English and Spanish. Lawrence leads the discussion. Charles shows up with a cast on his hand. There is a full discussion. We vote unanimously to strike on June 12 if the company and union do not agree to cancel the contract and hold a supervised vote on the company's offer.

The following morning I get a call on the speakers. The voice is none other than President Cruse. "*Dave Ranney, Dave Ranney, please report to the administrative offices.*" He knows how to pronounce my name at least. I think that if Charles were here I would pop in and tell him it isn't raining anymore. But I am nervous about this and feeling a bit intimidated.

"Be careful up there," one of the pumpers shouts as I make my way to the offices. When I enter I see union business agent Mason standing in the doorway of Maurie Green's office. Cruse's door is shut. No one else is in sight. Even the receptionist Lisa is not at her desk.

"Get in here, Rainy."

I smile. "You and Maurie switch jobs? If so, I can tell you that you definitely got screwed. I would bet you have better wages from the union than Maurie does here, and you don't have to work in a shit hole." After

I enter, he slams the door shut. Despite the bravado I am quite nervous. He is about my height but muscular. His upper body seems jammed into his baby blue sport coat. Someone told me he also used to be a boxer. Too bad I didn't bring Mr. Clean along.

"What I want to know is what the fuck you think you're doing stirring up all the niggers around here."

"You have no business referring to your own members that way. Some of them are my friends."

"I don't give a fuck what you think about that. If you guys go on strike you'll all lose your jobs and you'll have trouble ever finding another one."

"You should be ashamed to call yourself a union man." We are both shouting. I'm more angry than scared at this point. But before I can say more he suddenly grabs me by the shirt and slams me against the wall of the office. He then slaps me hard across the face and I fall against the office door. The door comes open and I stagger out into the hall. He follows, red in the face. I pull a pipe wrench from my tool belt.

"Get your ass back to your friends! You continue this and I might just put you on the floor for good," Mason shouts.

Suddenly I am aware that Cruse has emerged from his office. He puts a hand on Mason's shoulder and says in his smooth, cool, dead voice, "Not here you won't, Jim."

I go back to the shop floor. My face is bruised. Several workers see me and come running up. "What happened to your face, man?" I tell them. Four guys go charging up to the offices. Later they tell me that Mason was running down the stairs to the street when they got up there and they gave chase. One claimed he had thrown a piece of concrete through the back window of his car as he pulled away.

The word spreads, and there's a spontaneous walkout. Pumpers shut off the pumps but leave the product in the pipes. The machines are simply turned off in the middle of their operations. In short, we leave the plant in a big mess and gather outside in the rail yard. Some workers run home and call second and third shift people to tell them what happened. Soon Lawrence, Heinz, Charles, and some of the other second and third shift people show up. We decide to strike but wait to begin until the following morning.

Frank comes out and says he wants to talk to me. He takes me aside and tells me he is sorry about what has happened and that we are all getting screwed, but he has less than a year before he is due to retire, and if he walks out with us he could lose pension benefits (such as they are). Bill, Henry, and possibly John Logan are in the same boat. "I hope you understand, Dave."

"Yeah. It's okay, Frank."

I then go home as do the rest of the first shift workers. Jack comes to the plant during the second and third shifts and tries to talk workers who are still around out of the strike.

The strike begins on June 9 at 8:00 a.m. Workers from all three shifts show up. We begin to chant in both Spanish and English: "No contract, no work! No contrato, no trabajo!" Kingsley, Beth, and a number of our other comrades are on the picket line. They bring poster board and markers for making picket signs, but the workers have already made some signs of their own on pieces of cardboard they have dragged out of the plant. On one rail car there is a huge sign that says: "Strike Today!" Other signs: "It's a Strike!" "United We Stand, Divided We Fall!" "Get the Gangsters Out of Local 55!" "Together We Stand: Unity!" "We Have the Power!" "Before You Get the Shortening, Take the Racist Gangsters Out!" "Down with the Racists!" "Local 55 Unfair!" "No Money for Me, No Money for You!" and simply "STRIKE! STRIKE! STRIKE!"

The police are out in force as well—four squad cars and about ten officers.

Frank, Henry, Bill, and the Mexican lead man cross the picket line to boos and jeers. But no one interferes with them. At one point, Frank, Bill, and Henry come out. Frank is in tears. He tells us that he had been ordered by Cruse to come out and tell us to get back to work or there would be serious consequences. He told Cruse that he couldn't do that. It wasn't his job, and some of them he considers friends. "Then Cruse looks at me and says: 'You're fired, Frank. Get out!' All these years in the plant and just like that."

"We told him it wasn't safe for us to be in here work'n' with a bunch of people who don't know what their doin', so were all goin' home," Bill added.

"I think you'll get your job back, Frank," I respond.

"Maybe," says Frank. "But I told Cruse to go fuck himself."

I give Frank a friendly pat on the back. "Sorry this had to happen." Then the three old friends walk off together. The Mexican lead man appears briefly to try to close an overhead door that had been left open. He shouts something in Spanish. One of the Mexican workers runs up and slugs him. He stays inside from then on.

We start walking all around the plant chanting various slogans— some familiar and some that the workers make up. "Los pueblos unidos, jamás serán vencidos!" "The people united, will never be defeated!" "Walk and strike, walk and strike, cause things ain't right!" "No contrato, no trabajo!" Oscears begins to sing an old blues song that had a refrain where everyone can join in.

"Misery, misery," he sang.

"Misery, misery," we answered.

"Is what the Shortening is to me."

"Is what the Shortening is to me."

That's the chorus. There are a variety of verses all insulting and some obscene regarding the union officers and the company brass. Everyone is into it. At one point three union guys show up. All of the workers are shouting at them. There are police nearby. The union officers motion me over to their car. I go, but this time I am followed by about thirty guys.

"Hey, Mason," Charles shouts. "You want to try to put Dave down now?" They tell me the strike is illegal, and we will all lose our jobs if we don't go back immediately.

"You going to call these guys niggers to their faces like you did upstairs? You're finished here. We'll file a complaint with the international. And we'll go back to work once the company agrees to another vote. Not before."

Cruse also comes out. He is calm and conciliatory. "Hey guys, this is all a misunderstanding. I just want to make some shortening."

I respond, "We'll be back once you cancel the contract and hold another vote, Joe." *It is easier to mock him and call him Joe when there are thirty guys to back me up.* He turns and walks away.

Eventually, we decide we need to break the pickets down into shifts. Lawrence, Charles, José, and I emerge as the leaders. We hold a meeting and pass around sign-up sheets for each picket shift. We distribute our phone numbers, and everyone is told to call us if something comes down and we are not on the line. I notice that Heinz is beginning to play a lesser role. He is still huffing and puffing about sabotage, etc. but never really does much of anything except show up for his picket shift.

Around 6:00 p.m., a number of cars pull up and women begin coming to the line. They are bringing food. It turns into a big picnic. A Mexican woman takes a plate of beans and rice and offers it to one of the black workers. A black woman follows suit with the Mexicans and soon we are enjoying a feast of ethnic food. And I notice something else. There are a few six-packs of beer around but no shake 'n bake and no reefer. No one is intoxicated! That pattern will last for the duration of the strike.

★

For the next few days we hear that management is trying to produce shortening in the plant with supervisory personnel. But they have no way to load it and ship it out. We can see that the fill line is running and the cubes of shortening are piling up. The truck to deliver the cubes is in the warehouse, which is being picketed by three Mexican workers. One of these workers comes running up to where I am. He tells me that Maurie is in the warehouse and is planning to take a truck out. I look down the street to the warehouse. There is a police car in front. Three of us run down with the worker. Maurie is in the cab of the truck and is putting it in gear. I stand in front of the truck.

"Get the fuck away from the truck, Dave, or you'll get arrested."

Two more workers stand with me. He gets out of the cab and starts walking toward us looking like he wants to fight. Herminio, a very tall muscular worker, picks up a piece of two-by-four that is about six feet long and puts it over his shoulder. Maurie stops in his tracks, looking startled. Herminio asks me in, "Want me to use this, David?"

I laugh. "I don't think he is worth going to jail for, do you?"

Herminio smiles and puts the club down, much to Maurie's relief. Maurie gets back in the cab of the truck and I step in front of it just as he is about to go. I see him nod and two cops grab and handcuff me. I shout to the others, "Let this go. No more arrests. They can't move much with the truck, so it isn't worth more arrests." Someone translates for the other Mexican workers and they step aside, letting Maurie out with the truck.

I am taken to the neighborhood precinct station. It is one of the oldest police stations in the city. They have a bad reputation for abusing prisoners. I am scared as they march me in. A big cop, the watch commander, is sitting at a large opening behind a counter. The cops take the cuffs off and I am told to empty my pockets. They take my driver's license, and the sergeant copies the information on some forms. Then I am cuffed again, hands behind my back. The cops say nothing, but they are not particularly rough and are very businesslike. They march me to the other end of the room where there is a short dirty wooden bench against a wall. A metal pipe is attached to the wall behind the bench. They sit me on the bench and then attach another pair of cuffs to those that hold my wrists together. They clamp the second pair of cuffs to the pipe. I can barely sit on the bench. It is very uncomfortable. I remember needing to scratch my nose. Can't do it. Then everything feels itchy. One of life's little pleasures—scratching an itch—taken away, but that is as bad as it gets.

I am only chained to the wall for about a half hour before Kingsley comes in. He is followed by about ten of the shortening workers. They run right past the watch commander. They're making quite a ruckus as they come to where I am chained to the wall. They all start talking at once.

"Are you okay?"

"Do you need water or anything?"

"How about we bust you out of this shit hole?"

The police in the station are not happy. Kingsley goes to the watch commander and asks about charges. He comes over to me and the other workers and says that I'm charged with misdemeanor disorderly conduct. "It's not serious. They're goin' to allow me to bail you out now, so you won't have to go to the lockup. But I don't have any money on me."

The bail is only thirty-five dollars. The workers pass a hat, Kingsley files the paperwork, and they let me go. We make a triumphant return to the picket line.

★

The following day we hear that a large tanker truck is coming to pick up a load. We decide not to take arrests for this. The supervisors will run out of shortening or energy before too long. Heinz says he will follow anyone leaving the plant on his motorcycle and shoot out the tires. He brandishes a .38 pistol.

"Put that away, Heinz. If you really intend to do that, you're on your own," I say.

Other workers nod in agreement. I'm sure he's bullshitting, but having a gun on the picket line is inviting trouble with the police. Soon a whole armada of police cars and paddy wagons arrive and surround the loading bay. A large tanker truck then comes and pulls into the bay and one of the supervisors attaches a hose to the truck. Lawrence goes up to the truck and yells at the driver through the cab window.

"You really goin' to cross our picket line? Ain't you union?"

The driver is white. He is also big but looks scared. We try to look scary to him.

"Teamsters Local 179. They told us that this ain't a legal strike and we're not to honor your picket line. Sorry. I gotta work too."

We continue to harass him. In the course of this, one of the workers slips behind the cab of the truck and removes the pin that connects the cab where the driver is sitting with the rest of the truck. When the tanker is full and the hose removed, the driver puts his truck in gear and pulls out. The tank separates from the cab and comes crashing down onto the pavement. All the workers cheer and begin to dance in the street. The driver gets out of the cab and looks at the hitch without its pin. He is red in the face. "Fuck you guys!" he shouts. He starts to say more. I'm bracing for the "N" word. I can tell it is on his lips. But he looks around and thinks better of it. Instead he storms through the door to the administrative offices. He comes out ten minutes later and sits grim-faced in his truck.

It takes two and a half hours to bring heavy equipment that is capable of lifting the loaded tank and then maneuver the cab so it can be reattached. A new pin has to be sent for as the other was "lost." All the while we jeer and harass the trucker and the other workers who are trying to get the truck and its cargo back together. The whole thing lifts our spirits. A little act of sabotage goes a long way at no cost to us, because no one knows who took the pin.

The Chicago Shortening management decides that it is futile to try to run the plant without the labor and cooperation of their workforce. So they shut the plant down and send everyone but the top management people home.

★

As the strike goes on, the picket line is visited and joined by a variety of people. My own comrades and their friends are regulars. We are also visited by some of the other small communist groups. The Progressive Labor Party comes very regularly and passes out their newspaper that calls for "Revolution Now!" Some other groups do the same. We have a meeting to discuss how people feel about the support of these groups. A number of workers want to know what I think of the groups. I tell them I don't agree with all of their politics and that there are a few individuals coming who I know and don't like. The consensus coming from this discussion is that if anyone is genuinely supporting us we should not restrict what they say. So the communist newspapers keep coming.

At one point, Maurie comes out with a bunch of flyers. The flyers are urging us to return to work and threatening us if we don't. They also single me out as a "communist member of Progressive Labor Party." I tell the other workers that I am insulted by the Progressive Labor Party accusation. As for the communist part, they can make their own judgment. One of the Mexican workers comes to me and says, "Almost all of us from Mexico are communists, so we are fine with you." The black workers are not at all bothered by the flyer.

We are also visited by a group of Iranian student activists who are trying to depose the Shah of Iran. I had participated in their demonstrations against the Shah, so I know many of them. They march around the factory building with us, and later we get in a group and they explain their struggle in Iran. Lawrence says, "We are with you in this thing. That Shah sounds like a bigger motherfucker than the guy we got to deal with." There are handshakes and fists in the air all around as the students leave. Later some Puerto Rican nationalists come and explain their struggle for Puerto Rican independence. The picket line is becoming a school for a variety of political causes.

★

On June 16, the company files for an injunction against our strike in the Cook County Circuit Court. The union attorneys do not contest the move, but Kingsley and another lawyer, Val Klink, who is helping us, do. They petition for the case to be removed to a Federal Court on the grounds that the union and company are illegally colluding to deny us our rights under federal law. The judge denies their petition and dismisses them from representing us on the grounds that only the union attorneys have standing. He then issues a temporary restraining order (TRO) that prohibits us from picketing and sets a date to hear the company's motion on a permanent injunction. The TRO also orders all but six of us to return to work immediately. I am one of the six. So are Lawrence, Oscears, and Heinz. The ruling makes it clear that if we try to picket or restrict production we will face fines and jail time for contempt of court. If the rest of the workers do not return to work, they will also face contempt of court charges.

As the judge is handing down his TRO, a number of us go to the International Union Headquarters on the Near North Side of Chicago. We have signs that say, "Get the Gangsters Out of the Meat Cutters." We have called major media outlets, and they are filming our picket line and interviewing the workers. After a short period of time, a vice president of the International comes out and invites us in to talk. We had been trying to talk to the international officers all along, but they had refused until we "had exhausted our options with the local union." I guess they are now exhausted. I know I am.

As part of the Congress of Industrial Organizations, a section of the International had at one time been considered a "red union." The vice president who invites us to come inside may have been a member of the Communist Party during that period. He takes us into a large plush room, complete with thick carpeting and comfy chairs that are set around a long polished table. The workers look around the room decorated with portraits of departed labor leaders with some amazement, if not amusement. "Welcome brothers," the union man says heartily as we file into the room.

Lawrence responds: "Before we start, you got to translate everything into Spanish."

"Of course, brother." He walks out of the room and returns with a young Latina. She translates for the rest of the meeting. "I want you to know, brothers, that this is your union hall. It belongs to you, and we will do everything possible to work out this disagreement."

Oscears: "Does that mean that I can take one of these chairs home? I could really use one of these."

"These chairs are for everyone to use. If you took one home, your other brothers would have no place to sit." He addresses Oscears like he would a small child. He doesn't get the joke. Everyone else does, though. We are all laughing and some slap hands with Oscears. The union chief blushes and stammers on. We explain our case to him. There is another secretary present who takes notes in shorthand.

The meeting ends with no commitments except: "I'll see what I can do." That evening we meet to discuss the situation with the TRO and to report on our meeting with the International. The workers vote unanimously not to go back unless they take the six of us too. The following day Kingsley and Val meet with the union attorneys. They all agree to a proposal that everyone goes back to work, including the six of us, and that the issues we have raised be submitted to binding arbitration (meaning we accept what the arbitrator concludes). The company rejects this proposal out of hand.

An insider at the union hall slips me a list of other plants in Local 55. One isn't too far away. It's in East Chicago, Indiana. We prepare a leaflet explaining our strike and asking them to support us on the picket line. We promise to return the favor if they need help. We go to the plant and distribute the leaflet as workers are coming on and off their shifts. These workers seem scared of us. Many won't take the leaflet, let alone talk to us. As we are in a company parking lot, it isn't long before plant security tells us to leave. The action is a bust.

Production at Chicago Shortening is still halted in spite of the lack of a picket line. A number of us hang out at the Workers' Rights Center. A company representative calls our office and sets up a meeting with the six of us, their attorneys, the union attorneys, and our attorneys (Kingsley and Val). Cruse tells us they will take everyone back but Heinz and me. He will not agree to arbitration. I say nothing but am amazed that after all of this they are so racist that they honestly believe that the workers could never have pulled this off without the white guys. Lawrence, Oscears, and Mario are laughing. They get it. We all get up, including Kingsley and Val, and walk out. The meeting is over.

On June 22, many of us are in the Workers' Rights Center. One of our comrades, Lisa, is talking to two of the wives who are with us. Mario's wife Monica has their baby with her. We have word that the company plans to pull some of the loaded rail cars out in the next hour. The women ask Kingsley if the TRO applies to them. He says no, and they decide to block the rail tracks. Monica gets a water bottle and grabs an umbrella that is sitting in the office. They walk out of the office and down the street. Monica opens the umbrella to protect the baby from the sun. The weather is hot and the sun intense. She is carrying a diaper bag and a bottle for the baby. One of the other women helps her carry the stuff. We all march down to Chicago Shortening. Kingsley warns the men not to stand too near the plant. We stand across the street in front of Sonny's Restaurant as the women and baby go and sit on the railroad tracks. Spirits are high. Charlie Johnson (Superfly) and I are standing together joking about something or other. Charlie is wearing his signature street clothes.

Several squad cars of police soon arrive. Cruse comes storming out of the office. He is no longer the cool tanned iceman. He is red in the face and carrying a document. He walks up to Charlie and me, flanked by two cops and begins to shout as he reads from the TRO. "*I am charging you with contempt of court for aiding and abetting and fomenting this action in violation of the law* . . . blah, blah, blah."

Charlie and I are laughing, as is everyone else. Cruse has lost it. The two cops handcuff Charlie and me. I say to Charlie, the only one of the men arrested other than me, "You need to watch the company you keep." He laughs.

Cruse is still shouting and ordering the police around. "*Get these people off the tracks! Arrest them for trespassing on private property.*"

As planned, the women go limp. Two policewomen first pick up Lisa by her hands and feet and carry her to a squad car, handcuffing her before they load her in. Two more women police officers arrive. They take a second woman, leaving Monica to last. The baby is screaming as one of the women takes her. She also apparently needs a change of diapers. The policewoman shouts to the men, "Is the father here?"

Mario raises his hand. "Take your child, sir!" He does and the baby quiets down. Then Monica is carried to the waiting squad. Charlie and I agree to walk on our own. As the cop is leading me to the squad he whispers to me.

"Man, that boss of yours is really an asshole."

"Tell me about it!"

"I don't want to do this. Many of us are sympathetic with what you're doin'. We know what a shit hole this place is. We've been ordered by our superiors to make these arrests and keep order."

"Understood. No offense taken," I reply.

We are taken to the same police station as before. The women are given chairs to sit in with no cuffs. They are bailed out by Kingsley and Val immediately—misdemeanor disorderly conduct and trespassing. But for Superfly and me the contempt of court charges prove to be more serious. We are chained to the wall, just like I was the previous time. Only this time we are there for several hours. The police close off the entrance to the station so that the other workers are unable to communicate with us. After a while I see Kingsley. He comes over and explains that they are trying to decide what to do with us. The company wants us to go to Cook County Jail. The union is apparently worried about possible legal repercussions and want him to bail us out. I'm worried about Cook County. It is a dangerous place. I am also increasingly concerned that we may indeed be dealing with the mafia.

After about three hours a man in a jumpsuit approaches and without a word takes Charlie's cuffs off the pipe. With his hands still cuffed behind his back, he is led to a back room somewhere. Then around a half hour later the man comes back for me. He is a small wiry light-skinned black man. He has a heavily lined face with a perpetual sneer on his lips. I soon see we are going into the lockups. I see a police officer but not the one who arrested me. They take my cuffs off, and the guy in the jumpsuit (I learn he is a guard for the jail) orders me to put my hands against a wall. He then takes my watch, belt, and everything that is in my pockets and gives it all to the cop who puts it in a large envelope with my name on it. The cop then leaves.

The guard is now carrying a heavy nightstick. He pulls me away from the wall, takes the nightstick in both hands and gives me a hockey-style cross-check. He hits me hard enough to make me stagger. "*Move!*"

We are walking down a narrow aisle lined with small cells. Each cell has a toilet without a seat and two narrow benches. The cells appear to be about eight feet by six feet. There are frosted windows near the top of the cell with bars that let in a bit of light. They are filthy. There is a faint smell of disinfectant mixed with urine, vomit, and unwashed bodies. (I am hoping I won't have to shit while I am in here. The toilet is particularly nasty looking.) The walls of each cell are decorated with years' worth of graffiti—gang symbols, initials, hearts with xx loves xxx, crude drawings of nude women and sexual acts. Most of the cells are occupied. One has three people; most just one. With every step I take the guard uses the end of his club to jab me sharply in the back. If this is supposed to intimidate me, it is working well. I'm scared shitless. I believe the guard could be psychotic. He is clearly enjoying this exercise of power. I'm hoping nothing sets him off. I look desperately into each cell for Charlie. We get to the second to last cell and I see a young boy staring at me. He appears to be a teenager. We get to the next cell and to my relief I see Charlie. He is expressionless. He's scared too. The guard opens the cell door and gives me a hard push into the cell. He slams and locks the door without a word.

They have taken Charlie's hat and watch. He is still wearing his sunglasses. He points to them. "I told the cop they were prescription. He let me keep them. Wouldn't let me keep my hat. Those motherfuckers better not mess up my hat."

We talk about whether it would be worse to spend a night or two in Cook County or here. We agree that neither option is very good. We are sitting on our "bunks" facing each other. We hear a shout coming from the next cell, the one where the teenager is. *"What da'ya think you're doin'?"*

We hear sounds of a scuffle. Charlie tries to use his sunglasses as a mirror by holding them outside the bars to see what is going on. He is unable to see anything. Then there is silence. A while later we hear footsteps. We hear a voice. I think it is the guard. "Looks like he hung himself with his socks."

"All right then," another voice answers. "We'll take care of 'im."

We hear footsteps as the two voices walk away. Charlie and I look at each other. We both have the same thought. Charlie says, "I think the guard killed that boy."

"Yeah, me too."

A while later the guard is back. He unlocks the cell. "You, Rainy, you're bailed out."

"What about Charlie?"

"Him too. You come first. Get your ass out here." I look at Superfly. He motions with his head for me to go. I step out of the cell. The body of the dead boy is stretched all the way across the aisle. His eyes stare lifelessly at the ceiling and his mouth is open. There is a pair of white athletic socks tied together and draped around his neck. I look up at the bars on the window. I think there is no way he could have hung himself. I turn to Charlie.

"You're in good spirits, right Charlie?"

"Yes, I am."

"You're not going to try to hang yourself or anything?"

"No way, Dave."

The guard gets behind me and jabs me sharply in the back with his stick. "Don't step on our corpse," he giggles.

★

We are badly shaken by this. We learn the next day that the dead man's name was Dennis Lewis. He was twenty years old. He lived about two blocks from the Shortening plant. He had been arrested for a holdup that netted him twenty dollars. He was looking for drug money. Charles lives a few doors down the street from him and knows the family. Dennis Lewis's mother and three siblings live there. "I'd like to speak to his mother," I tell Charles.

"She's really fucked up, Dave. All of 'em is on drugs. She won't do nothin' about this."

"I want to try to help them, volunteer as a witness. Charlie will too."

"Well, okay," he says hesitantly.

We go over to the Lewis house. A small boy answers the door. Charles and I go into the living room. The mother and children are sitting listlessly in front of a TV in a shabby room with worn furniture and dirty dishes lying around. "What for you bring this white boy round here, Charles?" the mother says in a low voice that sounds more like a growl.

"He wants to talk to you about your boy bein' kilt. He was in the next cell with another guy when it came down. Thinks the guard killed him."

The woman explodes, jumping to her feet. "YOU LEAVE THIS THE FUCK ALONE! NOW GIT OUT BOTH OF YOUSE AND DON'T EVER COME BACK HERE AGAIN!"

We leave. As we walk back toward the Workers' Rights Center, Charles says, "They live by dealin' a little. They're not goin' to risk having the police involved in their lives." I nod.

When we get back we call the State Attorney's office, and I report what I saw. I am talking to an assistant. She gets the factual questions answered: when, where, what did we hear, what did we see. Then, "We'll look into it." When I hang up Charles says, "They won't do nothin'."

They didn't. The incident got a squib in the *Daily Calumet.* It quoted the Coroner's office saying it was a suicide. End of story.

A few days later I am riding with Lawrence, Charles, and Mario to attend a special gathering in an apartment in the North Side Logan Square community. The neighborhood is largely white and Puerto Rican working class. There are a lot of apartment buildings—eight-flat walk-ups. The neighborhood is beginning to gentrify. Many of the buildings have recently been sold and are vacant and under renovation. None of my carmates have ever been to this part of town before.

We were selected to represent the Shortening workers at a fundraiser sponsored by a comrade who lives in the neighborhood. Bill has invited a lot of leftists and liberals of various stripes to pay twenty dollars to hear about the Chicago Shortening Strike. The money made will go into our miniscule strike fund. We enter the apartment and it is packed with about fifty to seventy-five people. After a while Bill gets everyone's attention and each of us gives a short rap about the strike, with Kingsley explaining the legal aspects. We then mill around. My fellow representatives look lost and restless. We decide to leave. But I can't seem to find Charles. I finally locate him in a separate room. It is Bill's office. Bill is in the process of getting a degree in physics. The walls are lined with bookshelves full of books. Most of the books relate to physics and math. But there are other science books, as well as Marxist classics and a good collection of fiction. Charles is standing by himself in the middle of the room looking at one of the books. I am struck by the fact that he was perfectly sober—had no alcohol or reefer at the party or before. He is very still but turns slightly as I enter the room. "Man, all these fucking books!"

"He's a physics student."

"I don't even know what physics is."

"I'm not sure I do either, you'll need to ask Bill to explain."

"I can't make any sense of anything in these books." He is quiet for nearly a minute. "You know what, Dave? I sure as shit wish I could read all these books one day."

He is serious as he says this, looking me straight in the eye. But then he begins to snort and shake, ending in his infectious laugh. He slaps me on the back and goes toward the door. Still laughing he says, "Let's get the fuck out of here." I am laughing too but feeling very sad.

The following week I am ordered to appear in court to answer the disorderly conduct charge from my first arrest. Mason is also ordered to appear. His appearance relates to my complaint of assault and battery against him. Both charges are continued. Lawrence is present to be a witness for me. He is wearing a hairnet on his head. It is a style for many black men—actually a hairstyle. Before continuing the charges, the judge looks at Lawrence and orders him to come to the front of the courtroom. He mutters to me: "What the fuck?" then stands and walks to the bench. The judge lectures Lawrence about respect for the court and then orders him to remove the hairnet. Lawrence tries to explain that removing it would be disrespectful to him.

"Remove it or be held in contempt of court!" the judge shouts. He then motions to the bailiff who advances toward Lawrence who is literally shaking with anger. I am thinking that we may get into a fight right in the courtroom. At the last minute, Lawrence tears off the hairnet. His hair has been straightened and falls around his face in a tangle. He is thoroughly humiliated. He turns and walks out of the courtroom. After the judge continues the cases against both Mason and myself, Kingsley and I leave as well.

★

The strike is nearly broken. Twenty-nine of the original forty-seven strikers have been rehired. Charles is still out on disability. He has had surgery on his hand. Because he was on disability leave when the strike began, the company is forced to take Charles back as soon as the doctor clears him. Replacement workers have been hired to make up for those of us who have been fired. Without a picket line they are free to come and go. Production returns to normal.

We try to hold the group together. Over the July 4 holiday weekend we plan a picnic at the Indiana sand dunes park. Those of us who have been dismissed join the workers who have gone back to work. I realize how much we have come to like one another. Black and Latino, with Heinz and me representing the "white race," mix freely. It is a far cry from the social relations before the strike.

On September 8, we hold another fund-raiser. This time it is at a neighborhood bar called "Tino's Lounge." We design a flyer and produce it at the Workers' Rights Center. We call it "Disco Inferno." We put the flyers around the neighborhood. Tino donates the space, and we sell tickets at the door. Chico volunteers to be a DJ. As people come in he shouts into the microphone, "Screemin' Chico is stackin' the racks, talkin' shit, and swallowin' spit."

People are dancing and having a good time. This time most of the partygoers are neighborhood people—friends of the Shortening workers. James arrives with an entourage of black gay men, lesbians, and transgender people in drag. He is comfortable to be himself in this place. I have invited a Puerto Rican woman, Marta Rodriguez, to sing. She is both an accomplished folk singer and a militant activist in the movement for Puerto Rican Independence. In between numbers she says a little about the songs she is singing and the cause of independence. She tells of prisoners in the struggle held in U.S. prisons and how we are trying to gain their freedom. The songs and her discussion are in both Spanish and English. Her message and her music are well-received by everyone.

This time there is alcohol and reefer being consumed. It is a lovely evening until some neighborhood kids come in drunk and start a fight. One of them pulls a gun and fires a round. He is immediately disarmed and thrown out by our security people. But one person is hit on the leg. Fortunately, the pistol was only a .22 and the injury does not seem to be serious. But it puts a damper on the party, and we soon shut it down. The shooting is a reminder of a lot of the realities outside, including our own situation with Chicago Shortening.

★

There is a whiff of life left in the strike. Kingsley and Val file a suit in Federal Court against the company and the union for collusion to deny us our rights under U.S. Labor Law. Lawrence and I go to the law firms of both company and union to serve them with a copy of our complaint. When we walk into these offices we see rows of secretaries at word processors all typing legal documents for many different cases they have going. Our complaint is typed and mimeographed at the Workers' Rights Center by Kingsley, Val, and me. The law offices representing the company and the union both have a large number of lawyers working there. We have two lawyers. When I hand the complaint to the union attorney Ed Benn, he shakes his head in disbelief. I am buoyed by the knowledge that despite our lack of resources, the shortening workers, Kingsley, and Val are giving the company, the union, their two huge law firms, and possibly the mafia all they can handle. They never dreamed that we could put up such a fight.

I am thinking that what is driving this is not the legal expertise of Kingsley and Val, as good as that is, but the willingness of the workers to stand up and fight. As we leave Benn's office, Lawrence and I look at each other and smile. I shout over my shoulder to the union attorney, "See you in court."

At a hearing the following day, the federal judge takes jurisdiction of our case because of the pending lawsuit. In doing so he voids the

Temporary Restraining Order, and we are free once again to picket. We return to the Shortening with a triumphant, noisy appearance. There are some new picket signs, written with magic marker on cardboard, that say, "We're Back!" and "The Injunction Is Dead!"

We are on the railroad tracks—nineteen of us are blocking an engine from pulling cars full of product. It is blazing hot outside. Some of the guys are shirtless. The president of the company in a coat and tie approaches us flanked by cops in riot gear. Charles, Lawrence, and I are in front and walk up to greet them. A huge cop—the one in charge of this operation—joins the president. He is wearing plainclothes, with his badge and ID hung around his neck and a large pistol stuck into his belt. The engineer from the blocked locomotive, another huge white guy, is there too.

The president, Joe Cruse, is screaming at us. Once again, he seems to have lost control. *"Clear the tracks!"*

The cop is more controlled, almost bored, but very firm. He towers over all of us. I find him scary and threatening. In a clear voice that is just loud enough for all of us to hear, he says, "This is an illegal blockage! Leave or be arrested!"

Charles steps forward. He stands inches away from the big cop, intruding into his space. He tilts his head up so he can look the cop directly in the eyes. "All we want is a fair vote on the contract." Charles's eyes are piercing, his voice clear. "For us this is about how we are going to feed our babies, man. That's somethin' worth fighting for. Movin' us out of here ain't goin' to be easy."

Charles steps back a half step, then smiles his infectious smile. Cruse looks scared. The cop has softened his threatening stance. The engineer steps between the cop and the Cruse. "No way I'm going to cross this picket."

Cruse stammers and sputters. He turns to the railroad man, shouting once again, *"You have to; it's your job!"*

The engineer looks at Cruse. "I don't work for you. So go fuck yourself." He turns and begins to walk away, then turns back and smiles at us. "Give us a call when you get this straightened out."

There is stunned silence. Then one of the workers begins to play drums. All of us are cheering and jumping up and down. People are dancing right on the railroad tracks. Cruse appears to be in shock. Charles suddenly grabs me in a bear hug and whispers in my ear, "I ain't never hugged a white man before."

★

Two days later there is another hearing in the circuit court. The judge proclaims that until the lawsuit is settled the injunction will be in force. He issues a permanent injunction with severe penalties should we choose to ignore it. In late July, there is a hearing in the Federal Court on our lawsuit. We are asking for 125 thousand dollars each in damages. This excites everyone, but of course the odds are clearly small that we can win. Kingsley and Val explain this but suggest that we come to court to testify. We decide to take the Illinois Central train into the Loop. The IC uses the same tracks as the engine that pulls the shortening cars out of the rail yard. And there is a train station right across from the plant.

The nineteen of us gather at the Workers' Rights Center and march as a group to the Shortening. Workers inside see us and stream out onto the loading platforms to see what we are up to. We wave to each other and continue walking. I'm hoping that our audacity to approach the plant under permanent injunction conditions makes Cruse and the others nervous. But before anyone calls the police we turn abruptly away from the plant and enter the station across the street. There are turnstiles that take either coins or tokens for the ride. The first worker at the turnstile jumps over, and a disembodied voice booms over a loudspeaker: "*You must pay your fare! Do not jump the turnstile! You will be subject to a fine and arrest!*"

The worker places his hat over a camera that is set up over the turnstile and shouts, "Fuck you!"

Everyone begins to laugh as we all jump the turnstiles. Just then a train pulls into the station. The doors open and we pour on board. As we start off, the group becomes silent and looks nervous. Logan tells us he has never been on this train before and has never been outside of South Chicago. Others nod in agreement. Charles breaks the tension.

"Say, Mr. Clean, what do the ladies on the sun look like?" Mr. Clean does not answer but suddenly there is a lively debate about what ladies on the sun, moon, and various planets might look like. The train pulls into the loop station nearest the Federal Building where our hearing will be. We walk there in silence.

When we enter the building we see some Iranian students who had been to our picket line. They tell us they have a hearing scheduled as well. We explain what we are doing there. Then another Iranian walks up to us. He is holding a handkerchief over his hand, which is bleeding. Lawrence asks, "What happened to your hand, man?"

"There was a Savak agent outside. I called him out and he stabbed me."

"What's a Savak agent?

"Secret police. I recognized him and we had words." He looks down the hall. "There he is."

A small man in his twenties, wearing a dark suit, is looking at us. Lawrence, Charles, and a number of others run at him. He turns and runs out the door with our comrades hot on his trail. I'm wondering what will happen if they catch him. They don't. They are soon back. "Got away. Motherfucker lost us in a crowd of people. I'd like to see him pull his blade on us!"

The Iranians smile and thank the guys for their support. We get on separate elevators to go to our respective hearings. As the elevator takes off Logan goes down on his knees. He is perfectly sober, so I ask, "What are you doing, John? Are you okay?"

"Yeah, I am praying to the Good Lord that we come out of this little room alive." Everyone laughs, but he is serious. He has never been on an elevator before and is frightened.

At the hearing some of us are called to testify. Cruse is there and also testifies, as do our union "leaders." It is a good try, but the case is ultimately dismissed. Later that week all the charges against me, Charlie Johnson, and the women are dismissed too. Also dismissed are my charges against Mason. Our momentum is dwindling.

Charles Hayes, a black vice president of the Meat Cutters and Butcher Workmen International union, is destined to become a congressman. Today he is holding a large political conference at a South Side union hall on black civil rights. He is considered to be a major figure in the black political and trade union establishment. We stand outside the meeting hall and hand out an information sheet about our strike as people enter. We then walk into a large hall with high ceilings. It is full of black people sitting on folding chairs. Most of the men have on coats and ties and women are wearing dresses and heels. There's a stage in front that includes a podium with a long table behind it. At the table we recognize major South Side black leaders. In addition to Hayes there are two congressmen: Harold Washington and Ralph Metcalf. There are also two state legislators and a local alderman. Metcalf is famous not only as a highly successful politician but also as an Olympic athlete who had run with Jesse Owens. Washington would go on to become the mayor of Chicago. But at this point all of the black politicians are considered to be part of the Democratic Party "Negro machine" that is subordinate to Irish Mayor Richard Daley's machine. Hayes is the most powerful black trade unionist in the country.

Lawrence and Charles walk up front to try to speak to them before the program starts. Three very large black men wearing black suits complete with shoulder holsters for their weapons come to the front of the stage and tell Lawrence and Charles to sit down. At the start of the program, Hayes comes to the podium and welcomes everyone. When he is finished, Lawrence gets up from his seat at the back of the hall. "Mr. Hayes, sir, we would like an opportunity to tell the people here about how we are being mistreated by some of the officers of Local 55."

We are shushed by the audience and the three men in suits are off the stage and moving in our direction. Hayes continues, ignoring Lawrence's intervention. As I look at the menacing figures advancing toward us, Lawrence whispers, "These guys are packing heat and they ain't fuckin' around. We better get out of here."

We leave before being thrown out. Social class prevails over race that day. But in the evening we are contacted by one of Hayes's aides who sets up a meeting with him. We meet him in his office. He listens to our explanation, asks a few questions, and tells us he will look into it. A few days later Mason contacts us and says they are willing to meet and discuss the whole situation. The meeting is held in a second-floor conference room at a seedy looking hotel located just West of the Loop. Someone we have never seen before meets us in the hallway. He turns to me and says, "They want to meet privately with you, brother."

"We all want to meet," I reply.

"They want to talk to you first."

Charles steps forward. "This reminds me of the Saint Valentine's Day Massacre." He points his arms at us like he's holding a machine gun. "*Powpowpowpow.*" Then the laugh.

Lawrence: "Go ahead, Dave. If they bring out the guns we'll be right here and come to the rescue."

The guys are all laughing (nervously). The guy who tells me to go in isn't laughing and looks totally clueless about what is going on. I go in.

He comes with me and closes the door. Mason, Jack, and another local union official are sitting behind a table. Mason speaks: "State your case, Brother Ranney."

"Lawrence is prepared to make the presentation."

"We want to hear it from you."

"Too bad. I assume Charlie Hayes made you do this. Lawrence is just outside the door, as are some others who can help answer your questions."

He nods to the doorguy (maybe a bodyguard?), who swings the door open. The Shortening workers have been leaning on the door trying to listen and literally come flying in the room. They are all laughing. Lawrence takes a tape recorder out of a bag he is carrying and proceeds to plug it into a wall outlet. Jack speaks in his squeaky voice.

"No need for that, brother. We are all union brothers here."

Lawrence agrees and unplugs the recorder and puts it away. I find out later that he has a small-concealed recorder in his pocket that is turned on. Lawrence has a written statement that he proceeds to read. There are no questions. Mason asks for the written statement and says they will review it. He also informs us that the company has agreed to binding arbitration of our dispute, as we had suggested much earlier. Binding arbitration is doubtless another result of the Hayes intervention.

The arbitration comes a week later and is held in a conference room at the Federal Office Building. We walk in with both Kingsley and Val. The union and company are each represented by a lawyer. A trained arbitrator who is supposedly neutral states that he will hear testimony from both sides and attorneys will be able to cross examine witnesses. The union lawyer, Ed Benn, raises his hand and the mediator calls on him. "Since we are representing Chicago Shortening workers for the union, Mr. Clarke and Mr. Klink have no standing here. I request that they be excluded from the proceedings."

Lawrence jumps to his feet. "They don't represent us. They're in bed with the company and that's what this whole thing's about."

Lawrence is admonished by the arbitrator. "You are not allowed to speak unless called upon." Val and Kingsley try to object and are similarly admonished. "I agree with Mr. Benn. Mr. Clarke and Mr. Klink are excused. You may wait outside the room and your clients can come out to confer with you, but you are not allowed to be in this room or participate in the hearings." Kingsley and Val leave. We all object loudly but are shushed and threatened with exclusion if we disrupt.

The rest is a total farce. We are allowed to tell our side. Cruse then testifies for the company. We write notes and pass them to union attorney Benn as Cruse tells one lie after the other. Benn doesn't even look at our notes and puts them aside. We keep the notes coming and Benn gets angry and starts crumpling them up, tossing some on the floor. Benn does not contest any of the company testimony. We begin to disrupt the proceedings. The arbitrator shouts at us that if we persist he will call security and have us ejected from the building. There is further testimony from company and union. I send Benn a note telling him to put Mason on the stand and ask him if he ever referred to the workers as "niggers." Benn angrily crumples my note and tosses it on the floor.

At this point Lawrence jumps up. "The union attorney is not representing us. He refuses to ask questions we request."

Benn responds, "I'm asking all the questions that are relevant to this case." We disrupt and are threatened again. We walk out. We then start our train ride back to South Chicago in stony silence. John Logan breaks the silence. "If I had known what would happen when all this started I would still have done it. This has been the proudest time in my whole life."

Everyone nods in agreement. I feel like I am about to burst into tears. But suddenly Lawrence begins to laugh. We all look at him like he has gone mad. "There ain't no justice," Lawrence says, " . . . just us." Everyone smiles the rest of the way home.

The arbitrator's decision comes down a few days later. He finds our complaint without merit. The strike is declared illegal. He says that in his opinion there was a binding contract between company and union that was the result of a vote by the labor force.

Our legal options are at an end. Many of the workers are back at work. Someone from the company calls the Workers' Rights Center and says I can come back to the plant to collect my tools and clothes that were left there before the strike. But they tell me that when I do I must come up to the offices and meet with Cruse first.

I walk into Cruse's office. There he is sitting at his desk, with his beautiful horses, his children, and his beautiful wife (*in that order?*) sitting on the bookshelf behind him. He is back to his cool, bordering on cold, self with his tan suit, dead eyes, and tanned skin. He motions me to sit down. I sit. "If you hadn't fixed the vote, none of this would have happened," I say. He laughs. I go on. "Okay, you win, we lose. I am both quitting and being fired. I understand. All I ask is that you take everyone else back and we will let you alone."

"You have no basis to ask anyone anything here. We had a meeting this morning of the officers and supervisors and I told them they could nominate whoever they wanted back. On that basis I chose who I wanted." He laughs. "You had one vote by the way."

I am now feeling totally intimidated. I always did have trouble looking this guy in the eye. Now that we are defeated and I am alone with him I find myself staring at the floor. I say nothing further. He picks up the phone and talks to the secretary. "Tell Bob to come in and take Mr. Ranney to the locker room and then out of the building."

Bob comes in. We walk into the plant and go to the special whites-only locker room. He hasn't said a word as we walk, but when we get inside the room he speaks. "We had a meeting to see who we wanted back. I told them I wanted you."

"I heard. I figured that was you." I begin to gather up my stuff.

"They laughed at me. Look, if you see any tools or any other shit here you can use, go ahead and take it." I see a welding torch and some tips and put them in my bag. He smiles.

"I don't see how you can stand it here, Bob. You did warn me that Cruse is an asshole. But it's more than just him." We shake hands. I leave the plant and begin the walk back to the Workers' Rights Center.

A few weeks later, Kingsley and I are in the Workers' Rights Center. I am at the mimeo machine cranking out a leaflet for some steelworkers. I'm feeling depressed and worried about all the workers who lost their jobs at the Shortening. I'm staring at the beautiful mural on the wall as the mimeo continues to whirr. The mural shows a dark blue night sky with bright stars and a moon. Neighborhood buildings are silhouetted across the bottom of the sky mural. A young Mexican artist named Francisco painted it. He lives in the neighborhood and came into the office shortly after it opened and offered to paint a mural on a blank wall if we would buy the paint. Kingsley agreed. It was Francisco's first piece of public art. He would go on to do many more.

The telephone rings. Kingsley answers. "Workers' Rights Center."

The door to the street opens and a bit of the putrid air from both the steel mills and the Shortening factory wafts in. Lawrence enters slowly. He looks tired, somewhat stooped. I can see from his face that something is very wrong.

"What?"

"Charles is dead. Murdered on the job."

"What happened?"

"One of the scabs—Howie—stabbed him to death. Right in the Shortening it happened. Howie's in hiding."

I knew that the Shortening management was forced to take Charles back because he had been on disability leave when the strike started. Kingsley and Val had made sure of this. He had been spending his days in a sea of scabs. I heard from some of the former Shortening workers that he was stoned most of the time.

Lawrence explains: "Charles had been taunting Howie in the locker room at the end of their shift. They get into a fight and Charles beats the crap out of him. The next day when Charles was on his way to pump some product, Howie was hidin' behind a tank. As Charles walked by, Howie jumped out and stabbed 'im. Charles managed to get to the locker room. He sat down heavily on a bench and said: 'Howie stabbed me. We got to do somethin' about that boy.' Them was his last words. He fell off the bench and onto the floor, dead . . . We'll get 'im!" Lawrence's fists are clenched.

"Don't! Please. Let the cops get him." Kingsley has hung up the phone. Lawrence slumps heavily into a chair. The three of us sit and stare at one another.

★

Three days later Kingsley and I walk into the African Baptist Church—a small dirty brick building three blocks from the Workers' Rights Center. The church is packed. Kingsley and I and a few of our comrades are the only white people there. We try to sit in the back but are ushered up to the front row. Charles is in an open casket. The smell of flowers, perfume, aftershave, and sweat is overpowering.

"Don't he look marvelous," Bill says. "I've seen him look better," I think, but I say nothing. There is singing—beautiful and upbeat gospel. Men are stony-faced and tense. Women are openly sobbing. Some woman from the neighborhood begins to scream and faints. People lift her up. I feel a bit faint myself. My stomach is queasy. I look in the back of the church and see Maurie Green! My muscles tighten. Suddenly I am nearly in a rage. Before Kingsley can grab me, I am in the back of the church, joined by Lawrence and about half a dozen former Chicago Shortening workers.

I'm shouting, "What are you doing here, Maurie!

"I'm here to pay my respects."

"You got no respect for any of us and no business here!" Lawrence hisses. His voice is tense and seething with anger. "Now get the fuck out." He gets.

After the service, the workers are standing on the corner across from the Shortening passing around a bottle of shake 'n bake and a number of joints. This time I join them.

1978–1979: We Are All Children of God

I'm looking half-heartedly for another factory job. I go to one place advertised in the *Daily Calumet*—a small steel fabrication shop. There are about a dozen workers sitting in uncomfortable wooden chairs filling out applications on their lap. The receptionist tells me that they have filled the position but I can leave an application on file. I take an application and sit next to a Latino worker who is staring blankly at his application form. I realize he can't read English. He might not be able to read at all. I ask him in my terrible Spanish if he needs help. He nods. I translate the application and begin to help him fill it out. A young black man pops his head in the door. "I'm hearing they have jobs open at Inland Steel."

I translate this for the worker next to me. Then everyone gets up and rushes out the door. Steel mill jobs pay good money and benefits. I drive out to Inland Steel in East Chicago, Indiana—about a thirty-minute drive from where we are. It is near FAROC, where I had previously worked. I park in the visitor's lot and jump out of the car. I see some of the guys who were filling out applications with me about a half hour ago. We approach the employment office and see a long line of applicants. The line appears to be about a half a mile long. We get in line. After about an hour a woman in a business suit walks down the line handing people applications. She shouts as she moves down the line. "We have filled all the vacant positions, but you can leave an application on file."

I fill out my application and take it to a big box where people are dropping off their forms. This whole process has taken nearly three hours of driving back and forth, standing in the long line, filling out and dropping off an application. By the time I get back to the Workers' Rights Center it is late afternoon. I check in with Kingsley and then go home, having put in a day of job searching to no avail.

★

I go to the unemployment office to verify my job search activities. To qualify for unemployment compensation you must prove you are "actively looking for work." Chicago Shortening has not contested my compensation. I guess the lawyers have had enough of us. I check job listings with one of the clerks. She points out that there are openings for welders and assemblers at a factory called "Thrall Car." It is located in Chicago Heights, directly south of the Workers' Rights Center. But it is a longer commute than I've ever had before—about an hour's drive if there are no traffic jams. I get in the car and start to drive south.

I fill out another application. The employment office is adjacent to one of the three large buildings in the complex. Thrall Car makes railroad freight cars. I learn that they employ about two thousand workers. I have never been in a factory this big. I see a large yard piled with sheet steel and about eighty sets of rail car wheels and axels (called "trucks," as I later learn). There is a great deal of noise coming from two of the buildings. This time the secretary asks me to wait. She comes back in about thirty minutes and tells me they have accepted my application. I will start at seven dollars an hour and get a series of raises after I pass probation (one month).

I follow her into a small clinic. It has a window looking into the building. There is a beehive of activity on the shop floor. Huge machines are cutting steel plate by moving cutting torches across large sheets of steel. There are also presses that are bending the cut steel. Welders are busy welding pieces of steel together at a series of tables. A nurse gives me a very perfunctory physical that includes a hearing test.

There is so much noise in the clinic that I can't really hear the faint beeps that tell her if I have a hearing problem. "That's okay," she says. "We're in high production so I couldn't distinguish the beeps either." My physical condition is apparently not a big deal.

The secretary comes back in and asks me for a shoe size and tells me that she will have a pair of steel toe shoes for me when I report for my shift at 4:00 p.m. tomorrow. She asks if I have welding leathers. I say no, and she looks at me for my size and says they will be available as well.

"Is there anything else I'll need?"

"No, we'll supply everything." I find this a refreshing change from the other places I have worked. This is a major company. A supervisor wearing a white hard hat enters. He is a young Latino. He introduces himself as Danny. We shake hands. He hands me a grey hard hat and a pair of safety glasses.

"I'm goin' to give you a tour." We walk into the plant that I have seen through the clinic window. Danny explains, "This is where we make the parts for the cars that are being assembled in the next building."

The moving, bending, cutting, and occasional hammering create a constant din. The air is heavy with welding smoke. At one end of the shop floor I see a large truck bringing sheet steel from the yard into the factory through an overhead door that covers nearly one whole wall of the plant. Danny takes me around to the various operations and introduces me to some of the workers. There is a large banner that reads: "Congratulations to the Fab Shop!" Danny explains that there is a safety contest among the three buildings.

"We won this month!" Danny says. "Too bad you'll miss the free coffee and donuts at the end of the shift today." He then soberly tells me why they are having a safety contest. "Three months ago there were two workers killed in accidents." I look around anxiously. "When you're workin' you must always wear your steel toe shoes, leathers, safety glasses, dust mask, and hard hat. You can only take these off in the locker room. There are all sorts of hazards here."

I get a similar tour of a second building. It is the assembly shop where the full rail cars are welded together on a long assembly line. The third building is a paint shop and the place where all the welds are inspected. "If they find bad welds, some of us from fabrication are called over to grind them out and do them over."

Danny and I shake hands again, and I head home and prepare for my shift that will begin at 4:00 p.m. the following day.

The commute is usually not all that bad. It is entirely on an interstate. I am advised by other workers to purchase a cheap radio that has a CB receiver. The truckers broadcast information about speed traps up ahead and if there is an accident advise which lane to be in. I need to be at my shift a half hour early because of possible delays. Being late for a shift results in a warning. The contract with the union specifies that four warnings will result in dismissal. The union is a Boiler Makers local. It seems to be a decent union, unlike Local 55 at the Shortening. All the safety equipment provided by the company is the result of union negotiations. There is a vibrant grievance procedure and a fair system to bid on jobs with higher pay. (My starting pay of seven dollars is about twenty-three dollars today—not bad.)

Danny starts me training with one of the workers who runs a steel press. Most of the skill is setting up the machine for a particular part when bends in the thick steel plates are required. The rest is simply lifting a sheet of steel with a small crane and pushing it into the press—easy but boring.

Then I am moved to spot welding. A number of pieces of cut or bent steel are placed and clamped into a jig that temporarily holds them together forming a part for a rail car. The spot welder then applies enough spots of weld to hold the whole thing together so it can be lifted out of the jig and placed on a pallet. Forklift drivers then transfer full pallets to the welding tables for finishing welds.

I find that it takes some time to clamp steel pieces into place and also to put weld spots where needed. I am constantly lifting my welding hood so I can see where to put the weld. The finishing welders can weld the whole thing up much quicker, so Danny is pushing us all to speed it up. We cut some time off by removing our welding hoods and putting a gloved hand between the welder and our faces, looking away when we strike an arc. But by the end of the shift my face and neck are burned by the radiation—like a bad sunburn. I try tying a handkerchief over exposed skin. Eventually the company issues an edict forbidding spot welding without a hood.

The spot welders file a grievance through the union. We demand that they reduce the number of parts per hour we have to spot weld or hire more spot welders. The compromise is a handheld welding hood that gives us more protection than hands and handkerchiefs.

One day I get promoted. I am given a welding table and classified as a welder rather than spot welder. It was a position I bid on that is awarded by seniority. It includes a small pay raise. As spot welders we were given a box of welding sticks to use. For final welds we use a welding gun that is fed automatically by a fifty-pound spool of wire weld. I load the fifty-pound spool at the beginning of the shift. I go through approximately seventy-five pounds of wire weld in eight hours. If I work overtime I can go through one hundred pounds of weld. Overtime is frequent and mandatory. I am working 4:00 p.m. to midnight. It is not unusual for midnight workers to call in sick. When that happens, one of us is tapped for four hours overtime.

My shift includes a toxic mix of workers with conflicting identities. The majority are white and come from nearby communities in Indiana. Their towns are all white and are determined to remain so. There are also a number of black workers from Chicago's all black South Suburbs, including Harvey, Robbins, Dixmoor, and Ford Heights. The hostility between the two groups of workers is very high. There is even a segregated system of locker assignments. A partial wall separates the black and white sections of the locker room.

Added to the mix are a number of bible school students from a nearby Baptist college. I learn that management favors them. They are working their way through bible school and always side with management when there is any dispute. They always come to work on time and rarely call in sick. In return for their loyalty and punctuality they are allowed to practice their preaching on the shop floor during breaks. They have constructed an altar out of scrap steel that includes a large cross and a small podium that they move into the middle of the shop floor at break time. They use fifteen minutes of the thirty-minute break for a sermon and an effort at converting workers.

One evening I come into the locker room to eat my lunch, pull out my earplugs, and take off my dust mask. The outside of the mask is black from the welding smoke. When I blow my nose, my handkerchief is black. One of the preachers points to it and laughs. "Look at all of the vitamins and minerals we get on this job!"

"We should get better masks," I respond.

"Al is going to preach tonight. He'll be graduating soon. Why don't you give him a try?"

Curiosity gets the better of me and I grab my lunch and go out on the shop floor.

"When you go home tonight the roads will be icy. You could go off the road and meet your maker. What is he going to say? Are you ready to face judgment? Come down to this altar right here and now and give your soul to Jesus. It's that easy. Why take a chance on spending an eternity burning in hell? Why not receive God's blessing and spend that eternity in God's kingdom?"

I look around. There are about twenty workers there; most are white. Most are also bible students. I am standing with a few black workers. Suddenly one of the workers comes forward. He is crying. He is known as "Big John," a huge white guy with a bad limp and a well-known addiction to alcohol and other drugs. He had once been a professional football player but blew out both his knees before he could make it to the NFL. John kneels down before Al. He says in a loud croaky voice, "I give my soul to Jesus!"

"God be praised! Bless you John. You are a child of God. We are all children of God."

I go back to the locker room through a shower of a-men's coming largely from the bible students. My locker is next to Al's. Al comes in beaming. "We got Big John!" he exclaims.

"He was drunk and likely on heroin. You really think he's a keeper?"

With a crowd of white bible students around him, Al launches into a joke. "Hey guys. What's the difference between an all steel press and a nigger?" "The press moves."

Amidst the snickers, I ask, "Are black people children of God too?"

"Of course they are. Why do you ask?"

I look to the other end of the locker room. The black workers are looking at us. Mike, with whom I've been friendly, is smirking. He knows I am up to something.

"Hey Mike," I shout. "Why don't you and the other brothers join us. Al says you are children of God too." Mike laughs and walks in our direction. "Al just told us a joke that I'm sure he would like you to hear. How did that go, Al? Was it 'What is the difference between a steel press and a nigger?'"

Al is red in the face. He hisses, "Why are you doing this?"

Meanwhile Mike and the other black workers join us. "Because I want everyone to understand what a fucking hypocrite you are."

The black workers laugh just as the bell rings announcing the end of our break. I return to the floor with the black workers. Mike gives me a friendly push on the shoulder.

★

In January on a subzero day one of the truck drivers who has brought sheet steel from the yard into the shop drives out the overhead door as someone else is lowering it. He crashes into the door, knocking it completely off. We run over to see if it can be salvaged. It can't. A forklift comes and moves it out of the way so trucks can get in and out. The arctic air blasts unimpeded into the building.

Our welding tables are near the gaping door opening. My face, hands, and chest are hot and sweaty from the heat of the welding operation. My back, legs, and feet are freezing. By the end of my shift my feet are numb with cold. The fact that my job requires me to stand in one place, unable to move much and my boots have steel toes and a steel protective plate over my instep make the conditions even worse, as the steel in the boots sucks up the frozen air. In the locker room I take off my boots and try to move my frozen toes. One of the other welders comes over. "I have an idea," he says. "Be out on the floor early for tomorrow's shift. We'll make some heaters for our feet."

When I return the following day, I have an extra pair of socks and am out on the shop floor before the first shift is finished. My fellow worker has ten steel plates cut in twelve-inch squares, two pieces of pipe, and a bunch of smaller pieces of scrap steel. We weld the plates together into boxes that are open at one end. We use a cutting torch to make a hole in one plate big enough to stick the piece of pipe through it. We then pile some scrap inside the box. Danny the foreman sees us and comes striding over. "What the hell do you guys think you're doing?"

"Making ourselves more productive until the company fixes the door. When do you think that will be?"

"As soon as possible."

"Next June?"

Danny laughs. "Probably."

I connect the outside end of the pipe to a hose that is attached to a tank of acetylene that we use for torch welding. There is one of these hoses at every welding station. I crack the valve from the acetylene tank so gas escapes into the box. I then drop a match into my box and the gas lights. I have the box placed under my welding table near my feet. It works great, and soon all the other welders follow suit. Nonetheless, it is still very cold in the shop.

One day one of the welders turns on his gas and then gets engaged in conversation. By the time he tries to light his stove there is way too much gas. There is a loud explosion and the guy is burned. The injury is not severe, but he has to go to the hospital. The next day all the boxes are gone. Danny is passing out a memo from management forbidding the use of the gas to run makeshift heaters. But outdoor temperatures climb into the low thirties. This means I will likely get to keep my toes this year, but the cold conditions are miserable.

As the month continues, we experience another temperature plunge. Many of the workers on midnight shift begin to call in sick. Some quit. The result is that I am pulling a lot of overtime, working twelve-hour shifts. One night when I get off at 2:00 a.m. it is snowing hard and the temperature is in the teens. I am on the interstate when I spot a car pulled off of the road. A woman is standing next to it waving her arms. I pull off and walk over to her. What I see is surreal. She is wearing a light coat over what appears to be some sort of party dress, high heels with open toes, and no gloves. She is crying. "I don't know what to do. I have a flat tire and I don't know how to change it. I'm scared to be out here at night. I'm scared of you. Please don't hurt me."

She is practically hysterical and shaking with cold. (This is before the advent of cell phones.) "I can help. Open your trunk so I can get the jack and spare. While I'm changing the tire you can get in my car. It's all warmed up and you can thaw a bit. When I am done you can get back in your car. No one will hurt you."

She seems slightly reassured and sits in my car while I change the tire. After she is safely back in her car with the door locked she cracks the window. "Can I pay you something? I don't have much money but if you give me your address I'll send some."

"No need. Just do me one favor."

"What?"

"Don't drive around in the winter without boots, gloves, and a warm coat, and ask someone to show you how to change a tire."

"I was really stupid. It won't happen again."

We both drive off. By this time I am dead tired. I get off the highway at Stony Island. There is a traffic light at the end of the ramp. I stop and look at my watch—3:30 a.m. Suddenly I am awakened by a horn blaring behind me. I look again at my watch. It is now 5:00 a.m. I had fallen asleep.

★

I've been making a lot of money with all of the overtime but am exhausted all the time. I don't even get to the Workers' Rights Center very often. I rarely see Beth. She is asleep by the time I get home and is up and gone to work before I awake. When we do talk over the weekend I feel a growing distance. The job is not only hazardous to my health but to my marriage as well.

In the spring they finally fix the door to the fab shop. It is late April so I guess they feel they are ahead of schedule! I'm given a new job assignment. I move down to the other end of the shop to work with another welder on a large structural part for one of the cars. The piece is so big it can't be welded on a table. We each take an end and lay it over several steel saw horses, weld one side and then turn it over and weld the other side. When we are finished we place it on a large pallet for the forklift driver who will move it to the assembly building. We then lift the next piece to the saw horses.

My co-worker looks like one of Snow White's dwarfs, only taller—big ears, a bulbous nose, and a perpetual scowl on his face. He is known as "Grumpy." He is quite bent over. He's in obvious pain, wincing every time we lift a piece. He stops often, takes off his gloves, and rubs his hands. He tells me that the pain is everywhere—hands, feet, back, and legs. "Bad arthritis."

"How long have you worked here?"

"Twenty years."

"This is probably where the arthritis comes from. So, when will you be able to retire, Grumps?"

He laughs. "I'm only forty-eight!" I stifle a gasp. I'm forty and I thought Grumpy was close to sixty-five. Is this what I'm going to look like in another eight years?

As I drive home exhausted after a twelve-hour shift, for the very first time I am questioning my decision to leave academia and work on the factory floor. I may not be able to do this work much longer. The commutes to Chicago Heights, the forced overtime, the loud, smoky, and sometimes freezing conditions in the plant are weighing on me. Grumpy's revelation about his age has shaken me up. My trip from work to home nearly always involves a constant struggle to stay awake. The night I changed the tire was just the beginning. I think of the preacher's scare tactic: "If you are driving home tonight and go off the road . . ." Other than making money to live, there seems to be no reason to be here at all.

And I am surrounded by racists, many of whom consider themselves to be Christian preachers. That night on the trip home I vow to at least try to find something a little closer to home.

1979–1980: This Is What We Do!

It is July before I have a solid new job lead. I call in sick to work and put in my application for a welding position at a structural steel fabrication shop—Mohr and Sons. It's not far from Chicago Shortening. I can practically walk there from home. South Chicago is peppered with steel fab shops making everything you can imagine. Steel fabrication is a category of factory in the U.S. Census. They locate near steel mills so they can take steel directly from the mill to their shop.

Mohr is an imposing structure. I am guessing it is four times the size of FAROC, the centrifuge shop where I began my life of factory work. But all together it is a much smaller operation than Thrall. Next to the main building there is a large steel yard with row upon row of steel plates of various widths piled high. In the front of the building is an entrance that opens into a small office just inside the door. It has a window that looks out into the factory and a doorway that opens onto the shop floor. A woman hands me an application. I fill it out and hand it to her. She motions to a man standing in the middle of the factory floor. He is wearing a hard hat, shaded safety glasses, and a rough leather jacket. He comes over to the office and the receptionist hands him the application. He glances at it and introduces himself as Mike. He is a foreman and a retired Chicago cop. We shake hands. He takes me into the heart of the plant for an impromptu tour.

The plant is one huge room. It is incredibly hot and full of smoke and the flash of welding. The noise from sheets of steel being cut, bent, and ground is literally deafening. The working conditions seem like Thrall on steroids. The shop has a high ceiling with heavy steel beams that hold two huge overhead cranes. These are operated by two guys who sit in small cabs that are attached to each crane up on the ceiling of the building. On the shop floor I see two projects under way. One is the construction of what looks like an enormous cup. It is called a ladle and is used to hold molten steel before it is poured into areas where it can be shaped into plates, tubes, and rails of various sizes and shapes. The other project looks like a house made of steel plate that appears to be an inch thick. Plates that form the walls of the house are being welded together by about a dozen workers. One of the cranes is holding a plate in place as the welding goes on. The men are working on scaffolding that surrounds the structure. The foreman explains that this is where I will be working. He tells me I will need steel toe boots with metatarsal protection, a leather welding jacket, leather welding gloves, and leather chaps. I have all of this from Thrall. The company will supply a hard hat with a welding helmet attached. He tells me to report for first shift in the morning and he will train me to do the job.

I call Thrall Car and tell them I am leaving. I worked at Thrall for a little over a year. I come in on my first day feeling like a knight ready for a joust. I am covered from my neck to my toes in leather. The foreman gives me a time card and shows me the clock where I punch in. He also hands me my hard hat, welding hood, particle mask, and earplugs. I am told to wear a mask to filter the smoke from the welding at all times. Another guy comes in with me. Incongruously he is wearing a pink cotton dress shirt, jeans, and sneakers. The foreman asks where his work clothes are. He says he doesn't have the money but will borrow some tonight and get the clothes. The foreman just shrugs his shoulders and climbs with us up on a section of the scaffold.

He explains that we are making a vacuum chamber that is part of the steelmaking process. A rail car takes a ladle full of molten steel into the chamber we are making. Doors close on the chamber and a vacuum is drawn inside that pulls out any impurities in the molten steel. The welds must be perfect and will be X-rayed at the end of each shift to detect flaws. If there are flaws we have to grind the weld out and do it over.

He hands us each an electrode holder that workers call a "stinger." It is attached to a long heavy cable. The cable is apparently connected to a huge welding machine that is out of sight somewhere. He also gives each of us three boxes of heavy-duty welding rods and tells us where we can get more when we run out. This is the electric arc "stick welding" that I did at the Shortening and for spot welding at Thrall. But the size of the rods and the heat and radiation they emit is something I had never imagined. He explains that we are welding the seams between sheets of one-inch plate steel. The edges of the plates have been ground to form a bevel that we are to fill with weld. He cautions us not to touch the steel walls without glove protection. Not only is the steel hot to the touch, it is grounded and has a continuous electric current running though it!

I realize after striking my first electric arc that I am out of my league. The heat of the chamber walls and the electric arc cause sweat to run into my eyes. The shirt under my jacket is soaked in the first half hour. I stop to wipe the sweat out of my eyes and pull up the hood, being careful to look away from the other welders to avoid a "flash burn" to my eyes. I use a handkerchief to wipe my eyes. I absentmindedly touch the wall with a bare hand. Not only does it feel like I am touching a hot stove but I also receive a shock. I do this a number of times on my first day.

When we go on break I pull off my mask and earplugs. The mask is black with filtered smoke. I get a new mask. I am soaked to the skin with sweat and uncomfortable. Tomorrow I will bring extra T-shirts to wear under the jacket. I look at my fellow novice pull off his pink shirt and undershirt. The skin on his chest and arms is bright red. He is badly burned. His eyes water. I can see he's in pain. He gingerly puts his shirt back on and leaves the building. The foreman had to know this would happen. He didn't say anything! What an asshole. As newbies neither of us knew the strength of the radiation from this work. I never see the guy again. I hope he'll be okay.

★

The next day half of my welds have failed. The foreman gives me an electric grinder that I use to grind out the welds. I carefully weld them over. Each day there are fewer failed welds, but the work is the hardest I have done in my life. We finish four walls and a floor. The entire chamber then needs to be flipped over to weld a ceiling on the top. This requires the crane operator to lift the structure up about two feet and blocks are placed under one end. The foreman tells me to take the blocks and put them about four feet under the chamber. I look up at the crane operator. He waves and smiles. No way I'm going under there. One slip and I am flat as a pancake. I tell the foreman I can't do it. Someone else does.

The following day I come in to get my timecard. All the cards are on a rack on the wall near the little front office. I don't see my card. I stand there looking. I see the foreman and a few workers off a ways laughing.

The foreman finally walks forward. "I see you can't find your card. That's because you're no longer working here."

I realize this is his little joke to amuse the other workers. You let a guy who has been washed out minutes before his probation period is up humiliate himself before he is very publicly fired. I'm not only embarrassed, I'm angry—very angry. I pull off my hardhat and welding hood and throw it at him as hard as I can. He is startled as it hits him in the chest. "Pick that up and stick it up your ass," I shout as I walk out the door.

I'm now back to the business of job searching. I guess I can't use Mohr as a reference. During the following month I put in applications at eleven different places and visit another six that are not taking applications. Four are heavy steel equipment manufactures: automobiles, locomotives, tractors, and steel presses. Five are food processing: meat packing, corn products, flour milling, canned fruit, and candy. Two are smaller steel fabrication shops. Manufacturing jobs are getting hard to come by.

★

Finally, an application pays off. Beth is now working second shift at Solo Cup Corporation and has put in a word for me with her supervisor. The plant is a fifteen-minute drive from our apartment. It is nestled in an industrial park at 96th and Stony Island Avenue—right on the edge of the South Chicago community. The plant makes paper drinking cups. Initially I am classified as a machine mechanic. I work with a team of mechanics who are assigned to repair machines that break down. We are supposed to get them back on line as quickly as possible. Occasionally machines requiring extensive repairs are taken off line and rebuilt by a separate group of mechanics.

The plant consists of two very large spaces. Most of the space is occupied by three kinds of machines. They are all the invention of Solo Cup and are made in a separate plant on the North Side of Chicago. A cup-forming machine is a combination of a printing press that prints different designs onto a large role of paper, a stamping machine that stamps out what will be the cup itself, and a gluing unit that presses the pieces together. All three aspects of producing a cup have to be in perfect harmony or the machine jams up. Clearing jams and correcting the timing of the printing, stamping, and gluing are my main tasks. It is a complicated machine—lots of moving parts.

Once a cup is completed it is pushed into a tube and whisked across the plant with compressed air to one of two other machines. Cold drink cups go into a machine that sprays melted wax on them, cools them, and spits them out so that packers can gather them up in groups of fifty or one hundred, bag them, and pack them into boxes for shipment. The hot drink cups are made from a special paper and are sealed by a heat process in a different machine.

The other room contains rolls of paper, a huge air compressor, a fleet of forklifts, and a bailing machine that takes scrap paper—the cuttings from the cup-forming machine—and compresses it into bails that can be recycled. A separate group of mechanics deals with these machines, as well as with the forklifts that regularly break down. The plant also includes a machine shop and a welding shop where small parts for all the machines are fabricated and welded.

On my shift about two-thirds of the workers are young Mexicans, half of whom are women. The rest are mostly Eastern European immigrants, mainly a mix of Serbians and Croatians. There are some workers who identify as Macedonian. All of these identities are presently included in the nation of Yugoslavia, so I find it curious that few say they are from Yugoslavia. In fact, many of these workers are still fighting World War II, and there is great animosity between Serbs and Croats focused in part on their religions—Orthodox Christians and Roman Catholics respectively. A number of the workers had fought on opposite sides in the war. There are almost no black workers here. *Hmm, I wonder how that happened!*

The mechanics and machinists who fabricate machine parts have the highest pay and the easiest jobs. We only have to work if something breaks or we are running out of parts. Otherwise we are free to sip coffee in the lunchroom, wander around the shop and talk (or flirt) with people who are actually working, or help each other fix our cars, which we park in the loading bay when there are no shipments going in or out. The mechanics and machinists are all men, mostly European, although about a third are older Mexicans.

The next highest pay grade is the cup-forming machine operators, who are mostly a mix of Mexican and European men. Their main task is to keep ink and paper in the machine, put scraps into bins, and make sure the machine is running properly. If not, they summon one of us. Each operator is responsible for two machines. There are also forklift drivers who bring rolls of paper to the machines, haul and bail bins of scrap paper, and remove pallets loaded with boxes of cups for shipping. Finally, there are the tenders of the waxing and hot cup machines who do the packing at the end of the line. They work the hardest and are paid the least. They all seem to be young Mexican women. Beth, who works second shift, is the exception. The plant manager on my shift is a middle-aged Mexican, and many of the supervisors are either Mexican or Puerto Rican.

Solo Cup is a privately held corporation run by two brothers named Robert and John Hulseman. It is the largest paper cup producer in the world and has plants in a number of cities around the country. The founder of the corporation was Bob and John's father. The Hulseman family has patents on all the machines. There is no union in the entire corporation, so the job classifications, pay rates, and determinations of who is hired, fired, and where they work is solely up to the discretion of the brothers and the managers who work for them.

In my first month I sail through my probation period and get a raise. (Since there is no union, there is no contract or published wage scale.) I have no idea who determines my wages. I get $6.50 an hour (about $19 dollars today). It is a bit less than I had at Thrall and not much for what I do but adequate for my needs, and I am learning a great deal about mechanics by working on these unique machines. This is the best factory job I have had. The plant is clean as a whistle compared to my previous jobs. It is relatively quiet. There are few safety issues, and for me the work is easy. My supervisor is an older white man of German descent named Dutch. He is nice enough and reminds me a little of Frank at Chicago Shortening. Best of all is the fact that I am free to roam around the plant and make friends with some of the workers and learn about issues in the plant.

Wandering around the shop floor I learn of a lot of resentment about how jobs are assigned. Also, some individuals are given petty privileges in terms of break times. There are also divisions among workers. Here the divisions are based on gender and nationality, including the various Eastern European nationalisms. Beth and I spend a lot of time on weekends talking about these things. She also notes that she works a lot harder than I do and gets a lot less pay.

★

I am approached one day by both Dutch and the supervisor of the machine shop whose name is Lucky. I am changing the belts on one of the cup-forming machines. Dutch introduces me to Lucky, with whom I have a nodding acquaintance. "We could really use you in the machine shop," Lucky says, "And Dutch has agreed to let you move if it's okay with you."

I'm a bit taken aback that they are actually giving me a choice. "What would I be doing?"

"I've looked at your background. We need a plant welder and you're qualified. The last welder quit. You seem to have experience with the techniques we need. I will teach you to do anything you don't know. We may also ask you to work in the machine shop on parts fabrication if we are shorthanded. I'll teach you to run the mill and some of the other machines."

"That sounds good."

I have time to get to know Lucky and learn a lot about his background. First, his name is not really Lucky. I never find out what it actually is. He says he prefers "Lucky." He is Serbian and was trained in vocational arts in Yugoslavia during the Tito era. He considers Tito to be a "great man" who held a diverse country together and kept Stalin out. Yugoslavian communism is "different than what the Soviets have." Unlike many of the workers from Yugoslavia at Solo Cup, he refers to himself as "Yugoslavian." He is sad about the tensions among the various ethnic groups that make up his country. When a group of Croatians bomb his church (he is Serbian Orthodox) he is outraged and considers the whole thing "stupid."

Lucky is one of the most skilled workers I have ever met. His vocational training is broad. He is a machinist but also a welder, a mechanic, and can do many of the things a mechanical engineer would do in this country. His egalitarian attitude toward the rest of the workforce reflects his background in Tito's Yugoslavia.

★

The welding shop is attached to the machine shop. Both are surrounded by a chain-link fence. But the fence around my welding shop is covered by heavy canvas to protect other workers from welder flash. It has its own entrance gate. The canvas offers privacy if I want to read or talk to someone unseen. On the other hand, it is open at the top so it is obvious from the reflection off the plant ceiling if I am welding or not.

I am practicing some welding techniques that Lucky has taught me when he enters my shop. "The cups keep jamming up in the waxing machines. The girls who work the machines know the most, so we need to talk to them." We walk over to one of the machines, and Lucky asks the packer what the problem is. What strikes me is the lack of any sense of hierarchy as he interacts with the worker. As she talks he makes notes in a small notebook. He interviews several other packers.

After conferring with a number of workers we go back to my welding shop. He looks at his notes. "They all say the same thing. Wax is building up in the chute where the waxed cups come down. We can redesign that, and you can build it." On the same notepad he draws a design for a new chute. It is to scale without using any ruler or other measuring device. He writes the dimensions on the drawing, explains the materials we will use, which include aluminum. He teaches me how to weld aluminum, which I have never done. When the materials come I build new chutes for all the machines. They work perfectly.

★

I am constructing a steel burn box for one of the heaters on the ceiling of the plant. Most of the fabrication of the box is being done in my shop. As I work, I hear the door to my shop open. I stop welding and pull up my hood. It is one of the young Mexican workers. He drives a forklift. His English is almost as bad as my Spanish, but we have always managed to communicate. "Okay if I watch a while?"

"Cierto. Cuidado con su ojos. El fogonoso de la soldadora es peligroso." (Sure. Be careful with your eyes. The flash from the welding is dangerous.) I hand him a welding hood and he puts it on. Later he asks me if I can teach him to weld during his lunch breaks. I agree that I can do that if I am not on a job. He comes every day and soon brings some friends along. They want a skill. I tell them that ultimately they will need more formal training.

★

Lucky comes in and tells me there is a problem with the bailer and asks me to check it out. Scraps of paper are dumped into a big container and a hydraulic lift compresses the scraps by pushing them up an enclosure to the ceiling, where they are bailed with wire, lowered back down, and removed for shipment. The problem is that the lift seems to have punched a hole in the roof. Since the roof is metal, I decide to weld a patch on it. We clear all of the paper out of the machine and put a metal plate on the bailer and slowly raise it to the roof. I go up on the roof with another mechanic.

As I am looking at the bailer from the roof, trying to decide how to go about fixing this, I hear my partner exclaim, "Get a load of this!" He is standing on the very edge of the roof looking out on the rest of the industrial park where our building is located. I walk over to where he is standing. The entire industrial area is littered with little scraps of paper as far as the eye can see. When the hole opened up on the roof, the lift pushed scraps of paper up and out and the wind did the rest. My partner faces the scene and stretches out his arms as if he was addressing the multitudes. Then he shouts, "This is what we do!"

★

As my shift ends, ten Mexican workers come marching through the plant. They make themselves and the large buttons they are wearing visible to everyone. The buttons say "Plastic Workers Organizing Committee." They are passing out flyers. I don't really know any of them. They are all second shift workers. I take a flyer and begin to read it. The leaflet states that they wish to form a union in the plant. The union is "Plastic Workers Local 18 of the International Laborer's Union." The full name, I find out later, is "International Dolls, Toys, Playthings and Plastics Laborers, AFL-CIO." I've never heard of this union.

As I read, Dutch walks over to me and puts a friendly hand on my shoulder.

"Stay as far away from those assholes as you can."

"Who are the assholes, the workers or the union?" I ask him half in jest.

"Some of those guys are for sure. But I admit that I don't know most of them. And I've never heard of the union. But I do know that the company will come down hard on them and anyone who tries to help them, so stay away."

I stiffen a bit and go into legalistic mode, saying, "What they are doing is protected activity under the law, Dutch. They have a right to try to form a union, and we get to vote on it."

"Maybe. But this has been tried twice since I've been here. All the people involved lost their jobs both times. I just don't want you ta lose your job."

"Thanks for the warning."

I wave to Beth who is coming onto her shift and go home. When I get home, I phone a few friends who are knowledgeable about union matters in Chicago. One is very clear. "They are a mafia union, Dave. Be careful of them."

I think to myself: "Great! Another mob connected union." If the Plastic Workers are successful, this will be the third such union I have been in, if you count the Teamsters in Cleveland where I worked at the zoo during my college days. I wait up until Beth gets home from work. She says the whole plant is buzzing about this. She knows many of the organizers, as they work on her shift. I feel conflicted. This is an initiative by some young Mexican workers who are really getting screwed. Pay and job assignments are not based on seniority or even quality of work. Yet the union they picked is troubling. Beth and I agree that we need to back the union drive but play a low-key role. That proves impossible.

★

The next morning the company has its own flyer written in both English and Spanish. It is well written and slick. They derisively refer to the union as "This dolls and toys union." The tone is gentle yet condescending. They say that the people on the organizing committee are misguided and call on the rest of the workers to urge them to stop. They hint at the mob connections of the union and talk a lot about the "Solo Cup family."

The next union leaflet is equally slick. They answer the company by articulating the grievances held by many in the plant—especially arbitrary job assignments and pay scales. It is mainly directed toward the Latino majority in the plant. I learn from some management contacts that the flyers are being written by company and union lawyers. Kingsley informs me that the company law firm is a notorious union busting outfit. He does not know who the union lawyer is. As weeks go by there is a constant back and forth via leaflets. Then the company calls a meeting of all workers. We are divided into small groups and are summoned into the lunchroom.

The spiel is delivered by John Hulseman himself in talking point form. It goes like this:

- We consider all of you part of the Solo Cup Family, and we appreciate your work and dedication very much.

- Anyone who feels they are being treated unfairly should talk to me personally, and I promise to look into it and correct any problems.
- The union only wants your dues money. They don't care about you or your families like we do. They will force us to use their corrupt insurance scheme instead of what we give you in benefits.
- They know nothing about making paper cups. Their other members make dolls and toys.
- Pay and benefits must keep us competitive. Sweetheart Cup is breathing down our neck. The success of this union venture could mean the end of your job.

There are a few questions, then we are hustled back to our work stations as another group is brought in.

In the coming days, foremen visit all of their workers individually. The plant manager also visits workers, asking them how they intend to vote. The supervisors also seem to have their talking points. The Mexican plant manager focuses on the Mexican workers and talks to them in Spanish. My visit comes from Dutch, rather than Lucky. I tell him I am undecided.

As the vote date draws nearer, the rhetoric in the leaflets heats up. The company openly attacks the union and vice versa. But then something else happens. Workers start disappearing. The word is the plant manager is firing them, charging incompetence or insubordination after they are written up and harassed by the foremen. I am friends with one of the few Mexican mechanics. He says that Mexicans are being targeted. Beth has a similar observation on her end. Before long a third of the workforce is gone and those remaining are forced to run extra machines and work extra shifts.

I ask my friend Amado if he knows any of the people being fired. He says he knows most of them. They are from the South Chicago neighborhood. We decide to contact them and invite them to a meeting. Amado gathers as many addresses as he can by contacting some people he knows well. When our shift ends, we start going door to door.

★

We ring a bell and the door opens. I recognize the young woman who answers the door as a packer on my shift. Amado explains what we are doing and asks if we can talk to her. She invites us in. We go into a living room with a TV set and some worn but comfortable furniture. The room is clean and well kept. The woman introduces us to her parents and three younger brothers. We sit in a circle around the living room. I talk and Amado translates into Spanish.

"The law gives you the right to form a union of your choice," I tell them. I ask the woman what reason they gave for dismissing her. In her case she says that the plant manager told her that the company is forced to lay off workers due to economic conditions. "Did the union contact you yet?" She shakes her head no.

"I have a friend who is a labor lawyer. He can explain your rights better than I can. Basically, we think that if we get everyone together we can file a complaint with the government and force the company to take you back. We are holding a meeting at a place called the Workers' Rights Center. The lawyer will be there and we will come up with a plan of action." I hand her a flyer and give copies to her mother and father. It gives the time, date, and place of our meeting.

We have not contacted the union about this. Amado doesn't like the union, and they have made no effort to contact anyone who has been fired. Yet they continue with their efforts to organize the plant. The Workers' Rights Center has moved to a space on Commercial Avenue. It is on the second floor of a brick building. At the top of the stairs is a large open space filled with some tables and about 150 chairs. At the back of the room there are five private office spaces. Kingsley occupies one of them and can use the large space as a conference room.

We hold the meeting in the early evening. I call in sick, but Amado is working and is held over from first shift, so he is delayed. About fifty workers arrive. Some bring family members. I spot one of the union organizers. He does not look pleased. We stall for about twenty minutes. I then welcome everyone in Spanish and explain we are waiting for Amado to translate. But people are getting restless. I decide to plunge ahead. As I do, Amado enters the room. He is sweating and out of breath. I introduce him and we start.

We explain that we are proposing two kinds of group actions to get their jobs back. One is to file a claim with the labor board since the dismissals violate U.S. labor law. Kingsley speaks to this. The other is to leaflet the plant to tell other workers what is going on and encourage them to go forward with the organizing effort. I talk about the importance of trying to involve the other workers and of showing them we are not going to take this lying down. We get people to agree to leaflet each shift. Everyone gives Kingsley the information needed to file an unfair labor practices claim.

The union organizer approaches Amado and I after the meeting. "Why didn't you call us? We can help."

"You seemed busy with the organizing drive. You want to help pass out leaflets?"

"Sure."

The next morning I arrive for my shift "undercover." I confirm that my cover is blown the minute I walk in the door. The plant manager and Lucky are standing in the doorway. The manager tells me my services are no longer needed. I laugh. Lucky takes me into the locker room and then into my former shop so I can gather my personal belongings. When we are in the shop he pats me on the back.

"I've looked into this union," he says. "They're really bad. I expect you know that." I nod. "I really respect your guts and principles," Lucky continues. "If I didn't have a large family to support I'd be with you."

"I know that, Lucky. It's been fun working with you. It really has." We shake hands and move toward the door where I meet Amado who has also been fired. "You think there was a snitch at the meeting," I ask? We both laugh. Beth is fired when she comes in for second shift. She hadn't been at the meeting. She'd been at work. Guilt by association!

★

Kingsley and I pursue our claim with the labor board. We are assigned a case officer. She is a young lawyer and very enthusiastic about going after Solo.

I am invited to a christening party for the niece of one of the Puerto Rican foremen. He lives at his sister's home. The family is roasting a pig in the backyard. I recognize the grill. I made it at the plant—cut an empty drum in half, attached some legs made out of angle iron. I even built the rotisserie. I am wishing I had made one for myself before I got canned. There is live music. Amado is there too. He has a band, but they play Mexican music. We enjoy Ricardo's Puerto Rican music. Ricardo has put away a lot of beer and pulls Amado and I aside.

"I know a lot of shit. There are regular meetings with the plant manager. We're told to harass people so they quit or fuck up. They want the Mexicans out so the whites can vote down the union."

"Would you be willing to testify to that at a labor board hearing," I ask?

"Shit yeah! I'm tired of doin' their dirty work. I've screwed friends of mine. I need ta find another job though."

I get a call the next morning from Amado. He is excited. "I hear the plant manager has been fired. The word is he got into it with Hulseman. Didn't want to fire more people. So they fired him. I think we should pay him a visit."

"Do you know where he lives?"

"Yeah. I'll call 'im and set up a meeting."

His house is in the South Suburbs—a long ranch house with a mani-cured lawn. We ring the bell and he lets us in. The manager is a diminu-tive man—trim and about five feet six inches tall. He's wearing tan slacks, a dark blue sport coat, and penny loafers.

The living room is large, with thick carpeting and new looking furni-ture. There's framed Mexican art on the walls depicting romantic scenes of Aztec culture. There's a very large crucifix displayed prominently on the wall at one end of the room.

"I couldn't do it anymore," he tells us. "I feel really bad about what I've done."

"What did they tell you to do, exactly, and who told you to do it?" I ask.

"A couple of lawyers who work for the company came to my office at the plant. They said the best way to stop the union drive was to get rid of the people most likely to vote for it. They didn't say 'fire Mexicans' directly, but that was the point."

"We need you to testify at the labor board hearing next week. Maybe we can get your job back. If we win this based on your testimony, all will be forgiven with the workers as well."

He agrees and seems relieved. I tell him I'll call him in a few days with the exact date and time. We'll pick him up and take him to the hearing. Our lawyer Kingsley Clarke will go with us. The next morning, I call the lawyer at the labor board and tell her about Ricardo and the manager. She gives out a whoop.

"We've got those bastards this time," she exclaims! "I've been wanting to get them for years." (When I met her, she appeared to be just out of law school; so, not very many years. But never mind.) I can't wait for the hearing. Maybe even Beth and I will get back on. I actually like the job.

★

A few days later the union election is held at the factory. To no one's surprise the vote fails. Dutch's prediction that it will lose as it has in the past and a lot of people will lose their jobs seems to be coming true. But we still have the labor board. The hearing is coming up in a few days, and I decide to call the case officer to get the exact time and place. I am put on hold for a long time. "I've got some bad news," she blurts out before I can say anything. "We can't take this any further."

"Why the hell not? They just had a vote without a third of the labor force. We have two witnesses to a clear violation of U.S. law."

Her voice is low and shaky. She sounds like she is on the verge of tears. "I don't really know, Dave. My supervisor called me into his office and told me there would be no hearing; they have determined that the witnesses are not credible, and I am off the case. I'm not even supposed to be talking to you."

"Maybe you should look for another job too." We both hang up at the same time. I'm not ready to give up. Maybe there is another legal angle. Maybe we can get the manager and Ricardo to go to the media.

I call Amado and tell him the news. "There's more," he says. "Ricardo's in Puerto Rico. Some of his buddies told me that the company paid off his parking tickets and are helping him with delinquent child support. They sent him to Puerto Rico for the time being. Also, I have been calling the manager. He isn't answering his phone."

In the evening we drive to the manager's home. There is a light on in the living room. We pull the car into his driveway, get out, and ring the bell. As we do the light in the living room goes off. Amado yells something in Spanish but no answer. As we walk back to the car we peer into the windows of the garage door. We see a brand-new car.

"Look at that," Amado says. "A new car with company plates."

"I hope for the sake of his conscience he got more than a car. That's cheap compared to what he's done."

★

Amado is looking for work, and so am I. Beth has found a job out in the Pullman Community with Agar Foods. She's canning hams. Our relationship continues to cool. We are considering a demonstration at Solo to maybe get some media attention. But I get an unexpected call one day from the union lawyer. "I'd like to take you out to lunch," he says. "How about Berghoff?"

Berghoff is a really nice place located right in the Loop. I agree to a lunch date. I don't know what the lawyer looks like but he spots me as I come through the door. He is dressed in an expensive tan three-piece suit and brown dress shoes. He has the same tan skin and cool to cold demeanor as my former boss at Chicago Shortening. "You can have whatever you want on the menu. My treat."

I order a beer and I look down the menu for the most expensive thing I can find—lobster claws and crab legs with a rich chocolate cake for desert. We speak very little while I scarf down the best meal I have had in some time. Over coffee he begins to explain what this is all about.

"The struggle at Solo Cup is finished," he says.

"Perhaps. But I have a few more cards to play."

"No, I am telling you it is over." His voice is low, nearly threatening.

"I don't work for you or the union, never did. The union could have done more to help all of us who were illegally fired, but you chose not to."

"True you don't work for the union, but I think you could. The union leadership was impressed with the work you did at Solo—you and the Mexican guy. What's his name?

"Amado."

"Yeah, right. Well, the union local president would like to talk to you and Amado about the union. Do you think you guys could get there tomorrow morning at ten?"

"I'll ask Amado."

He writes a number on one of his business cards and hands it to me. "Call this number when you reach the Mexican guy and confirm. I think both of you will find it very much worth your time. Also, you do need to back off of Solo."

"Why do you care?"

"The workers there voted down the union affiliation. So that's the end of it."

His tone was firm and this time definitely threatening. Actually, there was no point defying him and his mafia union. We have played all of our cards. The dismissed workers were now scattered to the winds, looking for jobs. And they would be unlikely to return to some other action just to stick a thumb in the eye of the Hulseman family and the mafia.

Amado and I decide to see what the union wants with us. They occupy a two-story building on Erie Street. We walk into the building and are ushered to the second floor by a receptionist. The large room at street level contains numerous desks. They are all occupied by either clerks or typists looking very busy. The entire first floor is a literal beehive of activity. We climb the stairs to the second floor and are met on the landing by another secretary who welcomes us and asks us to be seated in a large carpeted conference room. She offers us coffee, which we accept. It is good coffee, freshly brewed. There is a window in the conference room that looks out on a parking lot surrounded by a chain-link fence. There is a fleet of maroon Lincolns visible.

The union president enters. We get up and all shake hands. He is short and stocky, wearing dark blue slacks and a white shirt open at the neck. He is wearing a gold chain and an expensive looking watch. "Welcome to our union, boys. I'll get right to the point. We think you both have a future as union organizers. The way you pulled together all those workers and launched a fight to get them rehired was impressive."

"Yeah, but someone paid off our witnesses and somehow got the labor board to back off without a hearing," I reply.

"We're aware of that. We all got our asses kicked on this one. But you got to learn when to fold, and then pick your future battles. We think you guys have a future with Local 18. We need good organizers who are bilingual. Dave, you have a ways to go on your Spanish but part of the deal is that we will send you to Mexico for language training for two months. With the base you have I'm told you will come back fluent."

He gets up and goes to the window. We follow. "We can pay you a hell of lot more than you got at Solo, $1,650 a month to start and raises depending on your organizing success. And you'll get full benefits and a pension. We have our own insurance company and run the pension fund. That's what goes on downstairs. Another part of the deal," he says, pointing to the Lincolns in the parking lot, "You'll each be issued one of these cars to use for organizing work, as well as for your own personal use, as long as you work for the union. You'll have a card that will get you free gas."

I look at Amado. He raises his eyebrows. I turn to the union president. "I would like a little time to think this over."

"Me too," Amado adds.

"That's fine. But I'd like to hear from you guys in the next day or two. There are others out there who would jump at such an offer."

We shake hands. We thank him for the offer as we make our way out the door of the conference room and down the stairs. When we get outside we both begin to laugh.

"If we take these jobs, Dave, I expect we would end up wearing concrete shoes and standing at the bottom of the Chicago River."

"Guess we better decline, then."

★

I see Amado a few times as we both search for jobs. He invites me to come to a gig his band has at a private social club in South Chicago. It is someone's birthday party. I enter the club and wave to Amado who is setting up on a small stage at one end of the room. He comes over to greet me, gets me a beer, which he draws from a tap at a bar at the other end of the room, and sees that I am seated at one of the tables that are set up around a dance floor. There are colored lights hanging on the walls, candles on the tables, and some low overhead lights.

Amado's band consists of two guitars, a bass, and a violin. The music starts. Amado is the lead guitarist and does most of the singing. The songs are a mix of traditional romantic music and wild Mexican polkas. Many of the guests are on the dance floor. Between songs someone shouts, "La Bamba!" The guests cheer and begin to chant for La Bamba. Amado complies, and his band does a rather good rendition of the Mexican folk song made famous by Chicano rock singer Richie Valens. At a break Amado comes over and sits with me. He shakes his head.

"Always La Bamba!"

"You do it well."

"I'm sick of it."

We talk about our times at Solo, and he relays news of mutual acquaintances. Quite a few have new jobs, but some are still out of work. Amado, himself, has landed a job. I tell him I am about to go for an interview at a chemical plant in Pullman. As I leave the party we shake hands. He joins his band and I go out the door of the club and into the street. I realize we will likely drift apart once we are both working again at different shops.

1981–1982: We Aren't Dogs, Cabrón

After the Solo Cup experience I am wondering if my factory career is at an end. And if so, will anyone let me back into academia? Jobs are getting scarce in South Chicago. Wisconsin Steel is gone. U.S. Steel Southworks and Republic Steel are laying off workers. This is causing a scramble for the jobs available in the neighborhood. I admit to myself that leaving the comfortable and secure confines of academia is beginning to look scary to me. Yet I am the son of a mother whose nickname was "mule." She was stubborn and persistent and much of that rubbed off on me. "Once you start something don't even think about quitting," she used to say. Working in factories, of course, was not what she had in mind. Yet here I am without a source of income in a declining job market. I stubbornly decide to push ahead by looking for another manufacturing job.

Prior to attending Amado's performance I go to the unemployment office and look at the listings. I find a possibility in the historic Pullman area of the city where the famous Pullman passenger cars were once made. A strike in 1894 against the company ultimately shut down much of rail transportation in the U.S. At that time Pullman was a separate town that housed the Pullman workers, making workers dependent on the company for all of their needs including housing, education, food, health care, and even religion.

I drive to apply for a job at a chemical factory at 108th and State Street. Pullman is now a neighborhood within the City of Chicago that has greatly deteriorated. Some housing and factory buildings have been restored, and it is a place where Kingsley and I regularly take visiting radical friends who are interested in labor history. It is about a twenty-minute drive from the Workers' Rights Center, but still far closer than

Thrall Car in Chicago Heights. Also, I discover that the plant is a half block from where Beth is working.

As I pull into the parking lot, the building that houses Foseco Corporation looks grim. The inside, as it turns out, is even worse. My thought is that I will try to hang onto this job long enough to find a way out of factory work altogether. At this point I only want the income. My skills have developed considerably since my first foray into the centrifuge shop in East Chicago, Indiana. I can weld, do basic electrical and plumbing work, and have some experience fixing pumps, motors, and shop floor machinery. I put my real job record down on my application, hoping they won't check references. The plant manager talks to me about my experience, and I can answer truthfully as long as I leave out the strike at Chicago Shortening, the Solo Cup union fiasco, and my short-lived disaster at Mohr. He hires me on the spot and gives me a tour of the plant.

Before going onto the shop floor he puts out his cigarette, hands me a mask, and puts on one himself. "I hope you're not too put off by noise and pollution," he laughs as he adjusts his mask into place.

He explains that Foseco makes boards and other products that are used in foundries and in the steel mills to insulate molten metals as they are poured into molds and formed into a variety of shapes. We enter the shop onto a balcony that looks out over the entire factory floor. At one end of the balcony there are four machines that look like giant food blenders. An operator is filling the machines with old newspapers and then pours in powdery substances from a number of bags along with water. He turns the blender-like machine on as I peer into it. He is producing a heavy slurry that looks like concrete.

"What are the chemicals?"

"Mainly silicon flour. It makes a lot of dust, doesn't it? This is why we all wear masks. You'll also need goggles if you're working near the blenders and in some other places I'll point out to you."

"Oh!"

The operator is wearing not only a mask and goggles but a white hoodie and gloves. He looks a little like Lawrence of Arabia ready for battle in the desert.

The plant manager shows me a series of offices with picture windows that look down on the shop floor. He grimaces. "Management."

"Oh!"

We go into a room behind heavy steel doors. There are two giant green machines that look like the bodies of dinosaurs. "Air compressors. Everything in the plant runs on compressed air. If these go down, the whole plant goes down. They're as important as electricity." He opens a cabinet on the wall. There are two giant tubes inside.

"These are heavy duty fuses. If the compressors go down this is the first place to check. If these are okay," he says, opening the door and pointing to some boxes on the ceiling, "check those. Be careful with this stuff. It's really hot—220 to 440 volts!"

"What are the fuses doing up on the ceiling?"

"Haven't a clue. Hope you never have to change them." He shows me a box that has spare fuses. "If you do need to change fuses, here are the spares. The ladder you will need to get up there is down on the main floor."

"Makes perfect sense," I say. He laughs. I feel we will get along okay.

The next day I come in dressed as a knight in not so shining armor, ready for battle. I am introduced to my fellow maintenance workers. Most, I learn, are Guatemalans who speak almost entirely in Spanish. The operators and cleanup workers are a mixture of white, black, and Mexican men and women. Most are men. The maintenance workers are busy installing some switches along what looks like a narrow-gauge railroad track. I learn that the slurry from the blenders is pumped into a huge tank in the floor. The tank contains an impeller that constantly stirs the mix until it is pumped into molds that are placed onto racks and loaded into a small rail car. The car is pulled by a conveyor into an enormous oven, where the mash is baked, removed from the oven, and loaded onto wooden pallets for shipping. Compressed air cylinders and conveyors drive most of the movement. The baked mash from the oven is shipped to the steel mills and used to process the steel in its molten state.

This operation requires fifteen workers. We are in the process of automating, after which only two will be needed. When the car passes over switches along the track, a computer activates cylinders, turns the conveyor on and off, lifts and closes the oven doors, and turns the oven on and off for the correct period of time.

As we finish automating the line, I am feeling bad for the workers who will be laid off. But after a few weeks, I see another dimension of automation. One of the two workers left after layoffs takes the baked boards off the racks and stacks them on pallets. He also stacks the empty racks using a small crane. It is backbreaking work. But worse than that, this man is completely tied to the pace set by the computer. During breaks I can see it is beginning to unnerve him. He sits by himself in the lunchroom smoking a cigarette, looking miserable.

One day he can't seem to keep up. Railcars full of boards are piling up. He has access to a "panic button," which can stop the process in an emergency. When he pushes it, a loud alarm goes off. When that happens men in white shirts emerge from the offices on the balcony. After the alarm goes off a few times a foreman runs over to where the operator is working. "What the hell are you doing?"

"This fucking thing is going too fast. I can't keep up."

"Do your job! If you can't do it there are plenty of people who can. I probably just laid one of them off!"

The operator is covered head to toe with protective clothing and a mask. I can't see his expression, but a few minutes later he presses the panic button again. The foreman is back, on the run. He is shouting. "What the fuck did I tell you?"

Suddenly the operator pulls a knife, grabs the foreman by the shirt. "Next time you yell at me I'll cut your throat!"

Within minutes two security guys grab the man off the line and disarm and handcuff him. They take him to the lunchroom to wait for the police. Workers on the floor look at one another, spontaneously begin to shut everything down, and go to the lunchroom. The foreman and a few management people I have never seen before come in and order us all back to work. The union steward, one of my fellow maintenance workers, speaks up.

"The line moves too fast for one guy. He just went nuts. You would too." He turns to the foreman. "Why don't you try a turn at this, Paul?"

After some back and forth, the steward, foreman, and the two management guys go up to the offices and are there for an hour before the steward comes back in with one of the security guys who takes the cuffs off the line worker. They and the steward go back up to the offices. When they come down they tell us the company is letting him off with a warning and promise there will be a helper on the line beginning the next shift. In the meantime, one of the cleaners will fill in as a temporary helper.

Possibly the white shirts that kept coming out on the balcony when the alarm went off could see that the job was impossible. But in addition, they knew there would be a huge delay if they didn't back down.

The next time production is shut down, I do it all by myself. On the main floor there are several boxes of circuit breakers for much of the electricity on the shop floor. I am told to wire a charger for the electric forklift machines into one of the boxes by adding a new breaker. In my high school shop class, we were taught that the first thing you should do when something goes wrong with an electrical appliance is to turn off the electricity. This simple safety precaution is not an option because it would mean shutting down production. It has to be done hot, and the box has 220 volts of electricity. Did I mention I am not an electrician? I have only had the night course in basic electricity while I was at Chicago Shortening and the admonition in high school shop class to turn off the electricity.

I open the box and look carefully at how everything else is wired and gingerly feed the wires into place and began to tighten them. One of the wires slips out of my hand and hits the inside of the box. There is a huge flash and a loud pop. The flash is so intense that it temporarily blinds me. I can hear alarms going off, and when my vision returns I can see the air driven cylinders and pumps slowly grinding to a halt. For a moment everything seems to be moving in slow motion and then not at all. Production is halted and space on the balcony for the white shirts is at a premium. I grab a ladder and run up the stairs to the balcony. I have to squeeze through a gauntlet of flabby men in white shirts and ties. "Gangway!" I shout at the managers as I push them aside to get to the fuses.

"What happened?" "What's going on Dave?" etc., etc., mixed with more than one "What the fuck?" as I sail into the compressor room and check the 880 fuses. They are okay. Then I am up on the ladder and prying the boxes on the ceiling open. There is a gang of the flabby men around the ladder. I change out two fuses and the plant hums back to life. I then retreat to the lunchroom, pull off my mask, take out my earplugs, and light a cigarette. I briefly think about reefer and shake 'n bake and wish I had some.

I am placed on third shift—midnight to 8:00 a.m. I have never had to work this shift before and find it extremely difficult. I come home in the morning and find I am exhausted but unable to sleep. By the time I get to sleep it is almost time to get up again. If I want to have any sort of a normal life on weekends I have to function as if I am working first shift. That is, I need to be awake and active first thing in the morning. But when the weekend is over, I am due back at work by midnight—Sunday night/Monday morning. I don't see how workers ever get used to this. Steelworkers and hospital workers often work "swing shifts." That is, they switch shifts every month or two. I ask some of these workers how they do it—how they ever get used to this.

"We don't. Swing shift workers are always short on sleep. You kind of learn to take catnaps when you can—at home or on the job." I am wondering how long I can last working third shift.

★

One night there is a spectacular accident at the plant. No one is injured but the whole plant is down. Some malfunction of the switches gives the wrong signals to the computer that runs the line. The oven is full of product stacked in two rail cars. The doors to the oven are closed. Suddenly the conveyor starts pulling the cars out of the oven. The cars crash into the door, knocking it entirely off. The cars inside tip over and trays of product are spilled all over the inside of the oven. Some of the rails are bent.

I run over, shut down the oven, and press the panic button to signal everyone to stop working. The few white shirts who are working at night run out of their offices, peer over the balcony and run back inside. (It must have been quite a sight from up there.) Maintenance workers from all three shifts are called in and, of course, management is soon on the scene in full force.

After all the maintenance workers arrive we walk over to the oven. Everything near the oven is still too hot to touch let alone work in. So we all go into the lunchroom and begin planning how to proceed. The union steward is the most experienced and he emerges as leader of this venture. We make a list of what needs to be done, in what order, and who will do what while the shift foreman paces around the room going in and out the door. Suddenly he comes in looking agitated. "When are you guys going to get going? Do you plan to just sit in the lunchroom all night?"

"We'll start when the oven cools down enough to work on it," our steward says.

"How long will that take?"

"We have no idea. Do you?"

After a while one of the workers, Ervin, goes out to the floor to check. As he comes back, the foreman comes in behind him and lets out with a loud whistle. Then he shouts, "You guys get out here and get to work and do it now!"

"We are not a bunch of perros, cabrón," (dogs, asshole) Ervin shouts. "I don't even talk to my dog that way."

We were about to go back out, but we decide to sit a little while longer. The foreman seems to be performing for the management people. He is angry and humiliated but slams out the door without a further word. Everyone laughs. Our leader claps his hands. "Okay perros, let's get started!"

We go out to the shop floor. It is still very hot in the oven. Even with heavy gloves we can't touch the steel walls. After a half hour we decide to break for ten minutes to get water. When we get back the foreman and several white shirt guys are standing there. We pick up our tools as the foreman speaks, "What did you think you were doing?"

"Takin' a break."

"You'll take a break when I tell you to."

The steward tosses a shovel on the ground. We all walk back toward the lunchroom, as our group leader shouts, "Fix the fucking mess yourself, then you can decide when to take breaks."

There is some whispering among the white shirts and the foreman. Then. . . "Okay, okay, just please let us know when you're breaking."

"Will do," our leader says. "We'll get this done a lot quicker if you just leave us alone." We walk back and begin working.

Eventually, we get the oven fixed and production is up and running.

Things at the plant go smoothly for a while. But I am unable to adjust to midnights. I bring in a note from a doctor advising that I should be put on an earlier shift, but the plant manager says that since I have the lowest seniority and no one else wants midnights, I have to stay on third shift.

One night when I arrive at work, the foreman tells me that the motor that runs the mixer in the large holding tank under the floor of the factory burned out. The tank was half full of the slurry from the giant blenders that had hardened before anyone noticed the breakdown. Second shift maintenance has replaced the motor but can't get the mixer to run as it is mired in the hardened slurry. The foreman tells me, "You will have to take the slurry out by hand."

My orders are to go into the tank with a pick and shovel, break up the slurry, and load it into five-gallon buckets. The buckets are attached to ropes and a forklift above the entrance to the tank is used to lift them up and out when they're full. I climb down a ladder someone has put into the tank. There is no light, so I have a small flashlight attached to my hard hat. It is hot and stuffy inside. And the toxic nature of the slurry means that I have to be completely covered and wear an extra heavy mask. It is hard to breathe. The forklift driver yells down, "Give a shout when you need buckets lifted." He disappears from view. I feel incredibly depressed. A few days earlier I had turned forty-two. Suddenly I shout to no one in particular, "Fuck! Here I am forty-two years old and shoveling toxic shit out of a tank in the floor of a factory building!" I am startled to hear another voice. "And a year from now, señor, you will be forty-three and still be shoveling toxic shit out of a tank in the floor of a factory building!"

It is Ervin. He has been down there the whole time, but I didn't see him in the dark. He is laughing. His teasing picks up my spirits. It helps that there are two of us down there. It takes practically the whole shift to remove the slurry and restart the mixer. But the incident in the tank, my exhaustion from lack of sleep, and Ervin's joke make me decide to leave Foseco. I have been there a little over a year. When I leave the next morning I say goodbye to Ervin and the other workers. It's time to leave this life behind.

I get a job as a community organizer with a tenants' union. The person who runs it reminds me of "the prick" at FAROC. After two weeks of being verbally abused I leave. I apply to some other organizations in the "not for profit" world, but they are suspicious of my leftie background, knowing that I was a professor who had worked in factories for the past seven years.

Now I am scared of the consequences of my decision to give up my tenure at the University of Iowa. I am out of money. Beth has moved out and is living in her own apartment. She later files for divorce. I try to start a home repair business, but I'm not really good enough to do that sort of work. Much of what I did in the factory doesn't translate to home repairs. I am getting a little frantic. I decide to try a comeback to factory work.

I know that major factories in the Chicago Area are now closing. I don't yet know why. Nevertheless, I make another major effort to get factory work. In a month of intensive job searching I file twenty-four applications at factories on the far Southeast Side of Chicago. I also visit another twenty-eight plants where applications are not being taken. In Each place I go I join a line of unemployed workers. My search is ultimately unsuccessful. The year is 1982. Economic crisis is the reality, with President Reagan assuring us that if we cut taxes and government spending all will be well.

★

My friend from Cleveland who acted as a phony reference when I was first searching for factory work is in town for an urban planning conference. She calls and tells me about a party at the home of a University of Illinois at Chicago professor of urban planning. "I'm going. Do you want to meet me there? We could catch up."

"Sure."

I hate parties. But she is an old friend. It will be nice to see her. The possibility of getting back into academia never occurs to me. *Maybe I have been out too long?* The address is on the North Side. When I arrive a man opens the door and introduces himself. "Hi. I'm Rob Mier, welcome."

I introduce myself, tell him of Janice's invitation, and we shake hands.

"I know your work."

"You do?"

"Yeah. Your urban planning textbook is still in use. A lot of people wonder what happened to you."

"Oh, *that* work!"

"Janice tells me you've been working in a factory for the last decade."

"Err, actually only seven years, although some days seemed like a decade."

"What're you doing now?"

"Looking for work. Factory jobs are getting scarce."

I spot Janice across the room and wave. Rob moves off and Janice and I catch up. She introduces me to some of the other people in the room. Many are academic planners like I used to be. They know of my textbook; wonder where I've been and why I have been working in factories.

Would I ever consider coming back to a university? *Just now that seems like a good idea!* As I leave, Rob comes over and asks if I would meet him for lunch. When we meet he tells me that in addition to being a member of the urban planning faculty he heads up a unique research center that works in lower income neighborhoods researching questions asked by the residents. Would I be interested in being part of that? I would.

A page has just been turned in my life, but I am still emotionally attached to factory work and the people I have met on various jobs. The experience of the last seven years will be an important part of me for the rest of my life. Part of this, I realize, has to do with people who are disappearing from my life. The first to go was Charles. His death hit me hard then, and it still does today. But others with whom I spent so many hours working on the factory floor have simply faded from my life. I often think of many of them: Lawrence, Frank, Jerome, Amado. Then there is Charlie (Superfly), with whom I spent one miserable day, first chained to a wall at the lockup, and then in a cell. Mario, Screemin' Chico, Oscears, James, Lucky, Ervin, Esteban, even Heinz flash through my mind. *What happened to them as factories closed and moved overseas?*

As both a leftist and an academic I inhabit a different world from these guys. While I was working at FAROC, Chicago Shortening, Mead Packaging, Thrall Car, John Mohr, Solo Cup, and Foseco Corporation I inhabited a unique space where I was simultaneously an outsider looking in and an insider looking out.

2015: Thirty-Five Years Later

Thirty-five years later I am with Kingsley in front of what had been the original office of the Worker's Rights Center. It has recently shifted from being a nail salon to a small café. A week ago it was the site of a prayer circle led by the priest of Immaculate Conception. This street has become a shooting gallery, a major hot spot for the rising tide of gun violence in Chicago. They were praying for the shootings to end.

The vibrant street life that we once experienced when walking down 88th Street is gone. Many of the stores, restaurants, and bars on Commercial Avenue are closed. The distinct unpleasant odor of smoke from U.S. Steel and fumes from Chicago Shortening is gone, along with the thin red dust that used to cover everything. And it is quieter (except when the shooting starts).

The Workers' Rights Center has been gone for thirty-four years. For a time, Kingsley practiced criminal and labor law in small offices located in the Loop. He eventually moved on to teach criminal justice at Northeastern University. At this point we are both retired. We drive over to an abandoned house just across the street from what had once been U.S. Steel. We move some old furniture sitting by the curb against a house that has recently been repossessed by a local bank. The Sheriff's Department has evicted its residents. We stand shakily on top of the furniture as we attach a large banner to the house that proclaims: "Say No To Lakeview!" As I pound a nail into the front of the house, I say to Kingsley, "Could we have ever imagined thirty-five years ago that when we reached our seventies we would be doing this?"

"This" was more than hanging a banner. U.S. Steel Southworks, which once employed twenty thousand people is now gone. All the buildings where steel was made on the six hundred–acre site were demolished years ago. Part of it is now a park. Lakeview is the name of an upscale development that is proposed for the Southworks site. The proposal is what urban planners call a "new town in town" with fancy condominiums, a shopping mall, restaurants, and a movie theater. We want to stop it because it ignores the plight of the people who still live in the area—a desperate plight. They will never be able to afford to come anywhere near "Lakeview."

The former residents of the house where we attach the banner had bought it with one of the "subprime" mortgages with ballooning interest rates. They lost the house in foreclosure. This has happened to many others who lived nearby. Transient squatters occupy many of the empty houses. Some houses have been the victim of fire and stand half burned down.

We take the car onto a special recently constructed roadway leading into the site of the former steel mill, from where it is possible to either enter the Southworks property or bypass South Chicago altogether. It is intended to be an access road to the proposed "new town in town." "Build it and they will come," as long as they can drive and have enough income! The road and the park are a building block for gentrification that will further marginalize the residents of South Chicago.

We park the car and get out and enjoy a beautiful view of Lake Michigan, which is now surrounded by parkland. Near the small parking area is an old slip where ore boats once unloaded. Neighborhood fishermen stand shoulder to shoulder trying to catch perch and trout in these once toxic (maybe still toxic?) waters.

We continue our tour of the once lively working-class neighborhood. There aren't many people on the street. We see a group of young men sitting on a bench at a bus stop drinking something out of a bottle in a paper bag (maybe "shake 'n bake"). We drive down to the building that housed Chicago Shortening. An electrical contractor now occupies the building. The distinctive white tanks are gone. The railroad yards where we made our stand during the strike are also gone. Sonny's Restaurant across the street is boarded up and rapidly deteriorating. I glance down 91st Street. The houses that remain are more dilapidated than ever. But the churches, including where I attended Charles's funeral, remain. Our tour and some research reveal that all of the factories where I worked except Thrall Car are closed.

Chicago Shortening is hard to trace. It appears they went bankrupt about five years after the strike ended. The factory property was empty and in a blind trust for years before being purchased by the electrical contractor. The union, Amalgamated Meat Cutters and Butcher Workmen and Local 73 were dissolved in 1979, when they merged with the Retail Workers to form the United Food and Commercial Workers Union. The International headquarters on Diversey Street where we picketed and entered its plush boardroom is now part of a hospital.

Thrall Car has changed ownership, but the production of rail cars continues and is going strong.

Solo Cup is still in business, but the factory on 97th Street is closed. In 2006, the Hulseman family was forced out of what had been a privately held family business. In 2004, they decided to buy out their main competitor, Sweetheart Cup. To do so they received funding from an investment firm, Vestar Capital, in exchange for seats on the board. The terms of the deal included the provision that Vestar would have a controlling share of Solo if the company ceased to make money. The Sweetheart deal caused them to lose money and Vestar demoted the Hulseman Brothers. They cut the salaries of Robert and John Hulseman from $1.1 million each to a few hundred thousand dollars. (Maintenance workers like me were making about forty thousand dollars in 2004. Machine operators and packers were making even less.) The Vestar board members stopped the Hulsemans from regularly hiring family members as consultants and paying many of them up to 250 thousand dollars. The company's profits could no longer be used as a piggy bank to fund unrelated things, such as Robert's wife's theatrical productions. This gives me some insight about why the Hulseman family fought the union drive as hard as they did. There was a lot at stake. In 2012, Vestar sold the company to Dart Containers.

Plastic Workers Local 18, the union that tried to organize Solo and that offered me a job, is still alive and well, but its president John Serpico was convicted of mail fraud and a kickback scheme in 2001. In announcing his conviction, the media described him as "a prominent member of Chicago's La Cosa Nostra." His crimes included misuse of union pension funds. The union attorney with whom I had lunch at Berghoff was also charged with racketeering, embezzlement, and arson. It was alleged that he attempted to burn some files that were wanted in the investigation. In spite of this he managed to get his conviction reversed on appeal. He is now practicing law elsewhere in the U.S.

Foseco Corporation is now a global company based in England. Its U.S. headquarters is in Cleveland, Ohio. The company has faced asbestos litigation based on claims that during the 1970s it ignored warnings about the health hazards of the asbestos used in its products and chose not to issue warnings to workers who made these products or those who used them. This litigation is ongoing. I don't know whether we used asbestos at the Chicago plant or not. I was told the main ingredient was silicone flour, which is also toxic and dangerous enough. The factory at 108th and Langley where I worked is now closed. It has been declared an EPA Superfund site due to toxins in the ground and the building. When I inspected the site recently, the building was boarded up and surrounded by a chain-link fence covered with heavy canvas. EPA records show that the site is "archived," meaning there is no clean up under way. Therefore, the building and the land around it are unusable.

The police station on 89th Street where I was once locked up is now a community center. What is left of the South Chicago population can get community services in the former police station and lockup (if they are funded).

2019: Reflections

Bring Back Middle-Class Jobs?

My irritation at politicians and some economists who advocate "bringing back middle-class jobs to make America great again" caused me to reflect on my own time on the factory floor some forty years ago. The height of manufacturing employment in the U.S. was in 1979 when 19.5 million workers, or 22 percent of the U.S. workforce, were employed in manufacturing jobs. In 1980, Wisconsin Steel in Southeast Chicago went down very suddenly, destroying more than three thousand living wage jobs. That was a year after the Chicago Shortening strike. After that the numbers and percentages of manufacturing employment tumbled. All the steel mills in Southeast Chicago are now gone. I began to experience Chicago's ultimate collapse of manufacturing employment in the 1980s when I found it increasingly difficult to find work. The Southeast Chicago and Northwest Indiana area, once one of the mightiest heavy industry production centers in the world, is a shell of what it was in the 1970s. Today only 12.4 million workers, or 8 percent of the national workforce, are in manufacturing.

But what do politicians, planners, and economists mean by "middle-class jobs?" The manufacturing jobs I had did provide a living wage, but my wages were not nearly as much as I had made as a college professor. They were not even in the middle of the span of manufacturing wages at that time. Yet they were much higher than wages for comparable jobs today. Unions have launched a campaign to "Fight for Fifteen." Fifteen dollars an hour is not enough for a family of three to live above the poverty line. My wages in the 1970s were enough to live reasonably well, and my fellow workers could support their families. Those wages and some of the health and safety laws and basic worker rights were the result of militant labor struggle. In the 1930s and 1940s, workers organized and made great advances in improving working conditions and worker's rights. But in the 1950s, organized labor traded labor peace for a share in the post–World War II prosperity, and as a result militant trade unionism declined. Furthermore, from the beginning, organized labor's capitulation benefited white male workers but largely left out black, Latino, and women workers. In the 1960s, the rise of the civil rights movements included a new round of labor militancy led by blacks, Latinos, and women. That is the context of the Chicago Shortening strike and other instances of shop floor militancy I experienced in the 1970s and early 1980s. But just as gains were being made by labor during this period, manufacturing began a precipitous decline.

The decline in manufacturing jobs was a deliberate strategy on the part of corporations around the world. They were responding to the fact that in the most developed nations of the world labor militancy, including the movements for civil rights, had cut into their profit rates to the extent that the entire global capitalist system was threatened. The response to that was in play even as we struggled in places like Chicago Shortening, Solo Cup, and Foseco. Beginning in the 1980s, there were technological advances that made capital highly mobile. Production process technologies made it possible to break up the production process and to produce pieces of products in different places. The big box containers and the new ships, trucks, and trains to move them made it possible for these places to be located long distances from one another. Computer technologies, robots, and now artificial intelligence not only automated production but offered innovations in inventory control to enable firms to get materials they used in production when they needed it ("just in time," or JIT). In the 1990s, there were institutional innovations to eliminate any barriers to the flow of capital around the world under the guise of "free trade." Finance became a highly profitable "product" during this period and was used to open up the nations of the world to manufacturing.

I soon learned that the collapse of manufacturing in cities like Chicago was a systemic response to a global crisis brought on by workers insisting on living wages and higher health and safety standards. Many of the sorts of jobs I worked in have been shipped to other parts of the world where standards for worker health and safety, as well as wages and benefits, are lower, raising the rate of exploitation for the working class. The so-called "trade" agreements make it difficult for nations to raise standards. Moreover, other jobs are now done by robots and computers that don't worry about wages or health and safety concerns. Production in many industries is up, with far fewer workers.

In my book *Global Decisions, Local Collisions* (2003), I described how the collapse of manufacturing in Chicago and elsewhere was devastating to both the communities and their working-class residents. Small and large factories were drastically reducing employment or closing all together. Living wage jobs were being destroyed and were not being replaced. People were losing their homes. Families were breaking up. Gang violence was on the rise. There were suicides. Today South Chicago, where much of my story took place, is nearly a ghost town compared to what it was forty years ago.

But it wasn't until the fall of 1991 that I fully understood that the collapse of manufacturing was both systemic and global. Moving jobs to areas of the world where wages were low and regulations protecting workers and the environment nonexistent was a way out of an ongoing global economic crisis. It was a new strategy on the part of those in control of global capitalism to accumulate needed profits. But it was implemented on the backs of those who made up the industrial workforce and their families. Most importantly it brought the advances made by the militancy of black, Latino, and women workers to a dead halt and pulled the rug out from under these workers, in fact, all workers.

What can we say about the mantra that we should "bring middle-class jobs back to the U.S. to make America great again"? My experience doing factory work in the 1970s and 1980s and my subsequent research suggest that these jobs were not really "middle-class" and they were hardly "great." The work, for the most part, did provide a living wage due to the bloody labor struggles of the past, but the elimination of factory jobs in the 1980s and 1990s wiped out the fruits of those struggles. The work itself, however, was brutal, unhealthy, dangerous, and caused serious environmental degradation. One former steelworker said to me that many factory and steel mill workers hated their jobs during this period. This observation was consistent with my own experience. The movement of these jobs to Mexico, Central America, Asia, and Africa has imposed that brutality, danger, and pollution on peoples around the world. I argued in 2003 that a global system based on high capital mobility was not sustainable. Time has proved me right. By 2008, a full crisis was resurfacing. I wrote about that crisis in my book *New World Disorder* (2014).

Presidents and governors can bribe a few firms to keep several plants in the U.S., but that will have no effect on the massive decline in U.S. living standards that has been underway since the 1980s, because that decline is part of how the capitalist system works today. The appearance of the wealth of the 1% at the expense of the rest of the world's people is also part of that system. The wretched condition of much of the world's population today and the degradation of the environment will not be improved by any tinkering with the functioning of global capitalism.

On the other hand, the rapid development of robotics and artificial intelligence offer the possibility that our needs can be met without anyone working in the sorts of jobs that prevailed in the 1970s. Nike spent the 1990s moving production around the world, seeking nations with the lowest wages and fewest health and safety regulations, and is now attempting to produce their athletic wear with robots. Their competitor Adidas is starting to use 3D printers to make its shoes. Under capitalism these technological advances will simply generate a surplus population that will lack the means to survive. But the new technologies also offer an opportunity to move beyond capitalism to a society without waged labor or social classes. In such a world, labor can become a meaningful, creative activity for all to enjoy and share. My experience in the 1970s and 1980s has enabled me to see the potential for such a world, and it has intensified my desire to help achieve it.

Racism, Race, and Class

Police violence against blacks, the white backlash to the "Black Lives Matter" movement, the rise of a neofascist movement where white people proclaim, "Jews will not replace us," while marching with torches through the University of Virginia campus, are testimony to the fact that the raw racism I witnessed and experienced on the shop floor forty years ago is still alive and well. When I first went to work in the Southeast Side factories I was a member of Sojourner Truth Organization (STO). My early political education about race came from STO. That included Theodore "Ted" Allen's two-volume work entitled *The Invention of the White Race*, which argued that the white race was invented as a "ruling-class social control formation." Noel Ignatiev (Ignatin), one of the founders of STO, has written extensively on the subject. He and Ted wrote a famous polemic within SDS in 1966 called "White Blind Spot." It argued that the priority of radical organizing must be mass action against aspects of ruling-class favoritism toward whites. Ignatiev quoted Marx, who wrote: "Labor cannot emancipate itself in the white skin while in the black it is branded." These perspectives informed my actions and attitudes on the job in the 1970s and 1980s. Since then, Ignatiev has modified his views, suggesting that at times white supremacy may conflict with the immediate interests of particular employers. Furthermore, a belief in white supremacy continues to serve the immediate interests of some white workers who are struggling to compete in a world with diminishing opportunities.

The lack of a biological basis for racial categories is widely accepted these days. We argued in the 1970s that race is a political project on the part of the ruling classes. Ted Allen stated: "White supremacy is the keystone of ruling class power, while white-skin privilege is the mortar that holds it in place." Ted Allen and Noel Ignatiev's work made intellectual sense to me. But when I began doing factory work, I discovered that I was naive about the extent of raw racism within the working class. I had never come face to face with this in a workplace. When I went to work at FAROC, located adjacent to a large concentration of African American homes, I didn't really question why all the workers were white. When I took the test to be a maintenance worker at Chicago Shortening, it never occurred to me that the test was designed to keep black workers from getting the job. Black workers at Chicago Shortening who had taken the test knew that that it had nothing to do with job requirements. They also knew that passing the test required a level of education they didn't have. A warm reception from a racist pipe fitter and an equally cold reception from black workers were critical to my own education. And that education was deepened everywhere I went—especially at Solo Cup, Thrall Car, and Foseco.

STO's analysis of the critical role of white supremacy made organizing against any forms of privilege a priority. While other radical left groups attempted to sidestep the issue in favor of promoting working-class unity ("let's tackle issues we can all agree on"), STO chose to confront white privilege wherever it appeared. In my work in the factories I saw firsthand how a racial division of labor was both the keystone and mortar of the U.S. factory system. Chicago Shortening and all of the factories I worked in were a microcosm of this aspect of the factory system. Day-to-day life at Chicago Shortening highlighted the complex interrelationship of class, race, and nationality. The physical dangers and possible health consequences of working at the Shortening, the lousy health benefits, the company's ties with the union, its use of police and the courts, the corruption that enabled the company to pollute the neighborhood and endanger workers were all both racial *and* class issues. All of this came to the fore during the strike. There was no room for a position, common on the left in those days, that tried to find issues that could unite the workforce without touching race and nationality. Once the strike was underway class issues and race issues became intertwined. As a result, divisions based on race and nationality evaporated in favor of class for the duration of the strike. This dynamic also appeared in other struggles I took part in at other factories. At Solo Cup and Foseco it was Latinos who were expendable, and it was Latinos who took the lead in organizing a class response to abuses.

At Chicago Shortening, black workers' stark experience with both class and racial oppression on the factory floor, combined with the rising civil rights movement, meant that they were attracted to other movements around the world led by people not classified as "white." The affinity that the black Chicago Shortening workers felt toward the Iranian movement to displace the Shah, the Puerto Rican movement for independence and socialism, and the Sandinista Revolution in Nicaragua are examples. The dual class and race oppression in the past also enabled them to play a leading role in resisting both company and union during the contract dispute.

For my own part, I came into these jobs viewed as "white." This was especially true with the rigged test at the Shortening. But my political education in STO led me to encourage and support acts of resistance I encountered on the shop floor. I saw the act of taking my breaks with black and Mexican workers as a repudiation of the minor privilege I had of a special locker room with comfy furniture and white companions. When I stood by Charles's side (quaking in my boots) as he told the company, the police, and the railroad that "moving us out of here ain't goin' to be easy," I saw myself repudiating white-skin privilege in a small way. The point was not missed by Charles. It earned me a hug!

With the collapse of the factory system in the U.S., race and class oppression take on a very different form. The invention of the white race and the use of white supremacy and white-skin privilege as the key mechanism of class rule are still fully in play but in a new context. In my book *New World Disorder* I argued that today's form of global capitalism based on capital mobility and phantom financial products is not sustainable. The financial crash of 2008–2009 is ongoing. The system is in crisis irrespective of the formal recovery from the recession. Claims on value generated by the entire global capitalist system are now greater than the system is capable of producing. Claims on value include the need for living wages, housing, schools, health care, and infrastructure, among other things. What it adds up to is that the system is unable to reproduce itself.

This is not the first time there has been such a crisis of value. In the past, these crises have produced nasty periods of churning and flailing, as businesses, governments, and people frantically sought a way out of the mess they were in. It is the same today. The notion that the crisis can be ended by "bringing back middle-class jobs" is ludicrous.

Today's churning and flailing is defining how the institution of white supremacy is playing out. When the factory system was in full force, black, Latino, and other workers who were not defined as "white" were initially excluded from most factories in entire industries where better pay and working conditions prevailed. As the civil rights movement broke this down, these same workers were given the worst and most dangerous jobs at the lowest wages within all industries. Today entire industries have largely left U.S. shores. In U.S. cities, black and Latino workers who cannot be gainfully employed are being contained, imprisoned, and sometimes even exterminated. Those unable to gain living wage jobs are contained within neighborhoods by police occupation—or they are contained in the nation's prisons. And sometimes they are exterminated with gun violence, either at the hands of police or each other. White-skin privilege is getting a bit thin, but for many it remains the "privilege" of not being contained or exterminated. That leads to the chant: "Jews will not replace us." It is also largely responsible for Donald Trump's presidency.

While changing its form, the class/race dynamic I experienced in the factories is still a system of social control and must be attacked as such. With globalization of capitalism, workers not defined as "white" are living and working all over the world. As a result, we are seeing the rise of xenophobia and the demise of class solidarity. In the U.S., "privilege" means staying out of prison and living in a relatively violence-free neighborhood in an "exceptional" nation. Fighting injustice as both a racial and class issue is still the priority for a movement toward a new society.

Human Nature and the Fight for a New Society

One response to some of my writings about the need for a new society is that my vision does not account for human nature. One person told me that the human race is "hardwired" in such a way that we can't do away with war or race and class oppression, citing the arguments made by some of the U.S. founding fathers and published in the *Federalist Papers*. In response to my reciting part of a Carl Sandburg poem in which a little girl remarks, "Someday they'll give a war and no one will come," another critic put it simply: "But war is the default position. It always has been and always will be."

Such views assume that something called "human nature" is an eternal aspect of the human condition. Author Marilynn Robinson, in her essay "Death of Adam," attributes popular views on the content of human nature to a combination of the Book of Genesis in the Christian Bible and the ideas of Charles Darwin. But the heart of the matter to me is the notion of "permanence" as developed by the writer Raymond Williams. My experience on the factory floor challenges the notion that "human nature" is what Williams would call a "permanency" and is therefore unchangeable. That experience also helped me begin to look at the question of both human nature and its assumed permanence in a different way.

In my book *Global Decisions, Local Collisions*, written twenty years after I left factory work and returned to academia, I challenge the notion of permanence.

> We create "permanencies" as a way to organize our lives, as the bases on which we live our lives day to day.... But there are times when personal development depends on the ability to break out of the various permanencies we have constructed for ourselves or society has constructed for us.

I explain the process of breaking out of the idea that human nature cannot be changed by drawing on dialectical philosophy. People have within themselves ideas that conflict or contradict existing definitions of human nature. A social struggle or conflict of some sort can unleash a process that seeks to resolve contradictions by smashing the prevailing definitions of human nature, opening the door to radical changes in the way we live and how we organize society.

> [T]he social change process has a "dual rhythm." Groups of people (a class, a race or a gender) whose self-development is similarly thwarted, will join together to combat and get rid of what is holding them back. That is the first negation that involves the tearing down of the old. Secondly, in the process of tearing down the old, people can begin to develop an alternative and participate in the creation of the new. That is the second negation.

Formulations of "Human Nature" have always been a powerful tool of rulers over the ruled. Notions of "Human Nature" have historically placed thought-limits on any kind of social change that might threaten the power of social elites. The prevailing definition of human nature at any point in history draws heavily on religion and science, which in turn become part and parcel of prevailing "ruling ideas." And all of these ideas, as well as a conception of human nature itself, have been enforced by the power of the state. Religion, science, and government are generated by and reinforce a conception of human nature that supports the rule of elites over the ruled. For this reason, part of any project to radically alter society must be to change human nature itself.

The starting point of my ideas about human nature was my time working in the factories of Chicago's Southeast Side. When I began working at Chicago Shortening, workers there had little consciousness of a common class identity. Race identity was dominant, and racist attitudes and behavior followed suit. White racism and enmity between blacks and Mexicans was raw and at times vicious. Most everyone displayed a sense of hopelessness that conditions at the plant and in their lives could ever be improved, and this often took the form of heavy drinking and drug use on the job. The company encouraged these behaviors, creating a white locker room, enabling blacks and Mexicans to have separate gathering places, turning a blind eye to intoxication on the job, and placing some rather stupid people in positions of authority. This demonstrates on a micro-scale the notion of "ruling ideas."

Once the strike began, all of this changed. The meaning of class and the potential of class solidarity became self-evident and behavior changed accordingly. Also, there were indications that had the struggle prevailed, new "permanencies" would have governed day-to-day behavior. I saw and participated in similar dynamics at Solo Cup and Foseco. Had the Chicago Shortening strike or some of the worker actions at Solo Cup and Foseco been part of a broader struggle for a new society, the changes in the workers could have become new "permanencies" and a new human nature.

Lawyers and the Courts

It has been my experience that many activists look to the law, courts, and lawyers as a substitute for action. My view has consistently been that the law and the courts are designed to protect the capitalist system so that reliance on the law becomes a limiting factor in any class struggle. From the beginning, the perspective of the Workers' Rights Center was that any legal aid we offered should serve not lead workers' struggles, and the Chicago Shortening strike was a textbook case of this perspective in practice.

The objective of the Shortening legal strategy was to offer a line of protection for the workers in order for them to pursue the objectives of the strike. Kingsley and Val knew better than to rely on labor law. They employed legal tactics solely to keep the strike itself alive while we were under attack. Lawrence summed this up best when he said "There ain't no justice . . . just us!"

A broad benefit of the strike was the demonstration of both the potential and reality of solidarity expressed as "just us." The strike exposed the fact that union, company, and government institutions were united in opposition to a class-based "us." In the course of the strike we were able to set up our own organization. We overcame the divisive aspects of race, alcoholism, and drug addiction in favor of solidarity. And we were given the opportunity to discuss broader issues—the revolution in Nicaragua, the struggle for Puerto Rican independence, the Iranian movement to replace the Shah. These discussions opened up the potential of broadening solidarity to include others. And the legal work enabled solidarity to flourish.

Immigration

Today we are witnessing a crackdown on immigrants without documents. Immigration Customs Enforcement (ICE) is snatching people off the streets, out of their homes, and off of airplanes. In the late 1970s and early 1980s, there was also a crackdown on so-called "illegal" immigrants. At that time the immigration agents worked for an agency called

Immigration and Naturalization Service. Latinos referred to them as La Migra. There were massive raids on factories, where workers without documents were rounded up and deported, mainly to Mexico. People were stopped on the streets, in movie theaters, and in other public gathering places. La Migra also invaded private homes.

Immigration crackdowns have historically served U.S. economic policies. Beginning in 1954, for example, a U.S. program called "Operation Wetback" was instituted. In the next three years, about 3.8 million workers were deported. Most of them had been involved in the "Bracero" program, which brought Mexican laborers in to harvest U.S. crops and then sent them back to Mexico. Some of the workers stayed illegally, so Congress initiated the crackdown. Labor unions played a major role in initiating and supporting Operation Wetback. The Bracero program was ended abruptly in 1964. This brought about a concentration of unemployed Mexican workers at the U.S.-Mexico border. The Mexican government, in cooperation with the U.S., established a new program allowing U.S. factory owners to build factories along the Mexican side of the border and avoid the higher wages and environmental and worker protection regulations that existed in the U.S. Known as the "Maquiladora Program," it was greatly expanded with the signing of the North American Free Trade Agreement (NAFTA) in 1994.

In the 1970s, when I was working in the factories, La Migra was in the midst of a massive crackdown on "illegals." This is what prompted Noel Ignatiev and the Workers' Rights Center to publish the pamphlet mentioned earlier titled "Since When Has Working Been a Crime." Our approach then was to attempt to promote a class-wide alliance that could resist the crackdown. The basis for such resistance was class solidarity. We coupled that with an information campaign that advised immigrants of their rights if they were stopped. We also provided contact information for legal help. This is the context of the small action I described at Chicago Shortening that thwarted a raid by La Migra. At Chicago Shortening, Solo Cup, Thrall Car, and Foseco there were a significant number of Latino workers. Divisions based on language and a presumption of illegality were used at all of these factories as a mechanism to promote division within the workforce. In each workplace struggle in which I participated, "legality" became an issue. During the union campaign at Solo Cup this question set Latino workers against one another and undermined efforts to appeal for unity when Latinos were singled out and dismissed unfairly.

Active resistance supported by legal assistance continues to be an appropriate priority for today's crackdown. But the emphasis needs to be on why an attack on immigrants is in essence a class issue.

Left–Wing Intellectuals in the Workplace

During the decade I was away from academia (1973–1983) I was a member of four different radical left organizations: New American Movement (NAM), Sojourner Truth Organization (STO), Midwest Action League (MAL), and News and Letters Committees (N&L). Most U.S. revolutionary organizations during that period were spin-offs of Students for a Democratic Society (SDS), and they all shared the belief that a worldwide revolutionary movement would result in some form of socialism. But we were deeply divided over how that would happen and what that socialism would look like.

Some looked to other nations—the Soviet Union, China, Cuba, North Korea, or Albania—as models for their groups. Some were even funded by China or the Soviets. Many sent members to work in factories. The organizations I belonged to were different.

New American Movement (NAM) was organized as a coalition of independent chapters, each with its own ideas about the nature of a new society and how to get there. STO had distinct politics that attracted me. I was working in NAM's national office in Chicago when I convinced STO to become a chapter of NAM. Later, when they left NAM, I left with them. What attracted me to STO were a number of specific ideas that were developed into pamphlets and were discussed internally in study groups. The pamphlets are archived at the site www.sojournertruth.net.

Briefly, STO believed that the Soviet Union and China were state capitalist nations. They were not socialist. We also had a strong critique of the Stalinist authoritarian party structure that many of the left groups were emulating. Second, we did not believe that U.S. trade unions offered a path to a new society. Their adherence to U.S. labor law, with workers' movements tied to contracts with corporations, actually held these movements back. Third, as discussed earlier, STO contended that the system of white supremacy needed to be challenged in order for the working class to unite and overthrow capitalism. At the heart of white supremacy was the fact that a segment of the working class was defined as "white" and given certain privileges that separated them from and gave them advantages over workers who were not allowed "into the club." We saw it as strategically important that "white" workers "actively and militantly reject their partial, selfish, and counterfeit interests." All of STO's political work was framed in these terms.

During the time I was in STO there was an emphasis on political work with those in the factories. It was believed that people who made useful goods could most clearly see the class exploitation inherent in capitalism and their own potential to construct a new society based on the motto: "From each according to their ability, to each according to their need." Members of many of the revolutionary left organizations were getting jobs in factories, and STO was no exception. But STO's approach to this work was unique in that it was based on its views of unions and white supremacy and was inspired specifically by the example of black workers who were forming mass worker organizations at the workplace that were independent of unions.

In 1978, after two years in STO, a number of us decided to leave the organization and form the Midwest Action League (MAL). Among the internal decisions and actions of STO that led to the split was a decision at a national meeting to de-emphasize factory work. By the time we had the strike at Chicago Shortening, I was part of MAL. However, we were unable to hold MAL together for long, and I eventually joined another organization called News and Letters (N&L).

News and Letters had very similar politics to STO but came from different origins. In the 1940s, the Trotskyist Socialist Workers Party (SWP) debated the nature of the Soviet Union. A small group within the party known as the Johnson-Forest Tendency did a detailed analysis of the Soviet system and declared it to be state capitalist rather than socialist. In 1950, they split from the SWP and formed their own organization. Johnson's real name was C.L.R. James, an Afro-Trinidadian historian. Freddie Forest wrote most of her life under the name of Raya Dunayevskaya. She was born in what is now the Ukraine and was a little girl when counterrevolutionaries drove her family into exile in the aftermath of the Russian Revolution. She settled in the U.S. but for a time was a part of Trotsky's inner circle during his exile in Mexico. James and Dunayevskaya broke over philosophical differences that had an impact on what a revolutionary organization should be doing. At that point Raya formed News and Letters to try to put her ideas into practice.

Both Raya and C.L.R. James have extensive writings. Raya's work can be found in her books but also in an archive www.marxists.org/

archive/dunayevskaya. C.L.R. James had a considerable influence on STO. During the time I was working in factories, I moved from an organization influenced by James to one founded by Dunayevskaya. But this had no influence on how I pursued my work in the factories. Their formulations about the significance of work within the factory system, the role of trade unions, the revolutionary potential of black mass movements, and the nature of white supremacy were quite similar.

The politics of STO, MAL, and N&L shaped how I approached my work in the factories and how I related to other workers. But I was not "sent into" the factories by any of these organizations nor were there any organizational goals for me being there.

Outside In and Inside Out

During my years living and working in manufacturing, I often felt that I was experiencing the conditions and interacting with the other workers from the outside looking in. But at the same time, due to my work in the factories and my associations with the other workers there, I was also inside looking out. It was a strange feeling, and it had a great impact on how I saw what was going on.

Even though most of my fellow workers had no idea that I had a college education and had been a university professor, that is what I was (and am). That meant that if a strike got crushed or I had an industrial accident I was likely to end up on my feet, as I eventually did. I often wonder what happened to Lawrence, Oscears, Mr. Clean, Amado, Grumpy, the racist preacher, Ervin, and the other young guys I knew at Chicago Shortening, Solo Cup, Thrall Car, and Foseco. Did they get other jobs? Did any end up with cancer, emphysema, or other disabilities due to the toxic work environment? And if so, did they get decent health care? And what about their children? How are they doing?

Inequality of opportunity based on race and education is what made me an "outsider" in my own head and at times to other workers. I too was extended privileges based on the color of my skin. I knew it and so did everybody I worked with. I also had the advantage of education that most people did not know about. But the advantages extended to me because I was white and my educational opportunities kept me from making lasting friendships with the other workers. At the same time, I was able to use my life experience and my knowledge of history and the economy to better understand what was happening on the job and see possibilities to change society and the world. I did my best to share such insights—not simply through locker room discussions or leftie newspapers and leaflets but through my actions on the job. And when I did share my thoughts and ideas on the job I was on the inside with my fellow workers looking out.

Because of my own dual status I tried to be careful not to initiate actions that would put others in jeopardy. But at the same time, I also tried my best to be supportive of those who were willing to take risks and to reinforce and expand on the best of the ideas and visions to come from people when they are in a struggle. All factory workers lived with very visible dualities that were often contradictory. Racism, nationalism, and selfish individualism all coexisted with class solidarity. A meek acceptance of feelings of powerlessness coexisted with militant class struggle. The grim reality of day-to-day life at places like Chicago Shortening coexisted with murky visions of what an alternative reality might look like.

John Logan expressed a different vision of life when he said that if he had known what would happen when we started the action at Chicago Shortening he would still have done it because "these are the proudest days of my life." Lawrence expressed a pathway to a new society when he joked, "There ain't no justice . . . just us." And the struggle brought out the best in Charles. He put aside alcohol and drugs and made common cause with everyone on the line—Mexicans, white boys, even a Nazi! And when we stood on the railroad tracks and he stepped forward he was able to articulate a class-based vision and determination in universal terms:

> For us this is about how we are goin' to feed our babies, man. That's something worth fighting for. Movin' us out of here ain't goin' to be easy.

This statement galvanized all of us, including the locomotive engineer who was standing on the other side of our picket line and refused to cross it, eventually telling our boss to: "Go fuck yourself."

Charles's words and his actions that day were an inspiration to me, and they still are. Despite the ultimate outcome, the militant stance and the idea that "feeding our babies is worth fighting for" was about much more. He was talking about both class and racial exploitation and oppression and declaring that we will stand together and fight for a different kind of world. Charles's words and our stand on the tracks are the way I will always remember him. And it is the place I come back to whenever I reflect on my time living and working on the factory floor.

As I remembered my experiences of forty years ago and wrote about them, I also realized how much all of this affected me emotionally. As I wrote about certain episodes I sometimes found myself in tears. I had a particularly difficult time talking to others about my interactions with Charles without breaking down. Charles's death traumatized me. I was not really a close friend of his. At times he was hard to even like. But Charles's life mattered. It mattered not only because he was black or because he was working class, but because he was a young man who had a family. "Feeding our babies," as he put it, was very real to him. He had two sons and a wife. I saw them on the picket line and at his funeral. There is a tendency to forget individual people when we put them into categories. Politicians and activists refer to the "black community," "the working class," "the middle class," or the "American people" as if the people within are all the same. An individual's racial or class assignment is important politically because it frames his or her experiences in terms of similarities to others and forms the basis for social movements. But it is important to understand that each individual within these broad classifications lives an individual life and has very specific needs, hopes, and dreams.

The dualities of being simultaneously black, working class, and a specific individual contains a certain tension that Marx called the "social individual." That tension can at times cause one to withdraw into an isolated world of drugs and alcohol. But at other times it can cause the same individual to step forward and declare that "movin' us out of here ain't goin' to be easy." My experiences on the factory floor gave me a concrete appreciation for the social and individual dimensions of society and the tension between them. The relationship between the social and the individual is what moves people to action. I discussed earlier what I learned concretely about race and class. I also gained some insight into the importance of the individual lives of other workers.

Charles represented for me something bigger than himself. In the preface to this book I stated that my motives for all of my political activism generally and my work on the factory floor specifically could be summarized in Marx's vision of a "society in which the full and free development of every individual was its ruling principle." Charles had a desire to engage in such self-development. He told me this after his accident when he thought he had lost his ability to draw. He told me this the evening in the library of one of my comrades when he said that he wished that one day "I could read all these fucking books." He told me this when he stood up to the company, police, and railroad and declared that he was ready to fight to feed his babies.

The individuals who make up the working class around the world are thwarted in these hopes and dreams every day. And they will be until we are able to band together and create a new society. Charles's death represented to me a terrible setback and the realization of how far we are from the vision of society where the full and free development of all is its ruling principle.

One might ask from the vantage point of 2019 whether our efforts some forty years ago made any difference. It is an impossible question to answer in these terms. My factory work certainly had an impact on me and the way I have lived the rest of my life. I have tried in this "Reflections" section to summarize a number of those impacts. I gained insights into how labor in a capitalist society is reduced to a commodity and see clearly the potential of a society where labor is a meaningful creative activity, rather than a commodity to be exploited. I gained insights into the nature of social class and its relation to race in today's world. I gained a greater sensitivity to the importance of individuals who make up those categories. I learned lessons about how people can change their outlook—change their very nature—in the course of a social struggle. I also learned firsthand about the usefulness and limitations of legal avenues to social change and the proper conduct of intellectuals and the organized left in changing society. Many of these insights were derived from the process of labor as I lived it day by day. Others came from specific experiences such as the Chicago Shortening strike, the effort to form a union at Solo Cup, and the shop floor actions at Foseco. Many of these insights came from the words and actions of individual workers as we worked side by side day in and day out.

It is true that the factory system in the U.S. today is only a shell of what it was in the 1970s. Factory work has been scattered hither and yon around the world. And there is no new society as we envisioned it. Sadly, the condition of the working class in the U.S. and around the world is actually worse than forty years ago. As a result, some may conclude that all of the insights that I gained were for naught. But I find it difficult to believe that I was the only one who was deeply touched by what I experienced. And if that is the case, they too gained insights from these experiences that could be passed along. As I write this, I am seventy-nine years old and will likely never know whether these insights have been passed along to a new generation of workers and radicals who can build on the collective insights of my generation and keep the struggle for a new society alive. But that is my hope, and that is why I think our efforts were worthwhile.

Acknowledgments

I am grateful for the help and encouragement of a number of people who commented on earlier versions of this book. They include Mari Anderson, Jim Barrett, Kingsley Clarke, Fritz Damler, John Garvey, Terry Henkel, Noel Ignatiev, Sarah O'Neill-Kohl, Paul Mattick, Lowell May, Mike Staudenmaier, and Patricia Wright.

About the Author

David Ranney is Professor Emeritus in the College of Urban Planning and Public Affairs at the University of Illinois at Chicago. He received his BA at Dartmouth College and his PhD at Syracuse University. Professor Ranney has also been a factory worker, a labor and community organizer, and an activist academic. He is the author of four books and numerous articles and monographs on issues of employment, labor and community organizing, and U.S. trade policy. Some of his recent essays and books may be found on www.david-ranney.com. In addition to his writing, he gives lectures on economic policy and politics and also finds time to be an actor and director in a small community theater. He is married and has a son, daughter-in-law, and two granddaughters. He splits his time between Chicago, Illinois, and Washington Island, Wisconsin.

ABOUT PM PRESS

PM Press was founded at the end of 2007 by a small
collection of folks with decades of publishing, media, and
organizing experience. PM Press co-conspirators have
published and distributed hundreds of books, pamphlets,
CDs, and DVDs. Members of PM have founded enduring
book fairs, spearheaded victorious tenant organizing campaigns, and worked
closely with bookstores, academic conferences, and even rock bands to deliver
political and challenging ideas to all walks of life. We're old enough to know what
we're doing and young enough to know what's at stake.

We seek to create radical and stimulating fiction and nonfiction books, pamphlets,
T-shirts, visual and audio materials to entertain, educate, and inspire you. We
aim to distribute these through every available channel with every available
technology—whether that means you are seeing anarchist classics at our bookfair
stalls, reading our latest vegan cookbook at the café, downloading geeky fiction
e-books, or digging new music and timely videos from our website.

PM Press is always on the lookout for talented and skilled volunteers, artists,
activists, and writers to work with. If you have a great idea for a project or can
contribute in some way, please get in touch.

PM Press
PO Box 23912
Oakland, CA 94623
www.pmpress.org

PM Press in Europe
europe@pmpress.org
www.pmpress.org.uk

FRIENDS OF PM PRESS

These are indisputably momentous times—the financial system is melting down globally and the Empire is stumbling. Now more than ever there is a vital need for radical ideas.

In the years since its founding—and on a mere shoestring— PM Press has risen to the formidable challenge of publishing and distributing knowledge and entertainment for the struggles ahead. With over 300 releases to date, we have published an impressive and stimulating array of literature, art, music, politics, and culture. Using every available medium, we've succeeded in connecting those hungry for ideas and information to those putting them into practice.

Friends of PM allows you to directly help impact, amplify, and revitalize the discourse and actions of radical writers, filmmakers, and artists. It provides us with a stable foundation from which we can build upon our early successes and provides a much-needed subsidy for the materials that can't necessarily pay their own way. You can help make that happen—and receive every new title automatically delivered to your door once a month—by joining as a Friend of PM Press. And, we'll throw in a free T-shirt when you sign up.

Here are your options:

- **$30 a month** Get all books and pamphlets plus 50% discount on all webstore purchases

- **$40 a month** Get all PM Press releases (including CDs and DVDs) plus 50% discount on all webstore purchases

- **$100 a month** Superstar—Everything plus PM merchandise, free downloads, and 50% discount on all webstore purchases

For those who can't afford $30 or more a month, we have **Sustainer Rates** at $15, $10 and $5. Sustainers get a free PM Press T-shirt and a 50% discount on all purchases from our website.

Your Visa or Mastercard will be billed once a month, until you tell us to stop. Or until our efforts succeed in bringing the revolution around. Or the financial meltdown of Capital makes plastic redundant. Whichever comes first.

Strike! Revised and Expanded

Jeremy Brecher

ISBN: 978-1-60486-428-1
$24.95   480 pages

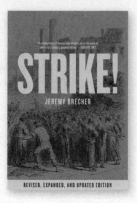

Since its original publication in 1972, no book has done as much as Jeremy Brecher's *Strike!* to bring American labor history to a wide audience. *Strike!* narrates the dramatic story of repeated, massive, and sometimes violent revolts by ordinary working people in America. It tells this exciting hidden history from the point of view of the rank-and-file workers who lived it.

In this expanded edition, Jeremy Brecher brings the story up to date. Revised chapters covering the forty years since the original edition place the problems faced by working people today in the context of 140 years of labor history. A new chapter, "Beyond One-Sided Class War," presents the American mini-revolts of the twenty-first century, from the Battle of Seattle to Occupy Wall Street and beyond. *Strike!* is essential reading for anyone interested in the historical or present-day situations of American workers and serves as inspiration for organizers, activists, and educators working to revive the labor movement today.

"An exciting history of American labor. Brings to life the flashpoints of labor history. Scholarly, genuinely stirring."
—New York Times

"Splendid… clearly the best single-volume summary yet published of American general strikes."
—Washington Post

"One of the most important books on labor history published since World War II."
—Howard Zinn, author of *A People's History of the United States*

"A magnificent book. I hope it will take its place as the standard history of American labor."
—Staughton Lynd

"Brecher's stories are interesting and exciting, his prose colorful, his quotes well chosen."
—Texas Observer

Wobblies and Zapatistas: Conversations on Anarchism, Marxism and Radical History

Staughton Lynd and Andrej Grubačić

ISBN: 978-1-60486-041-2
$20.00   300 pages

Wobblies and Zapatistas offers the reader an encounter between two generations and two traditions. Andrej Grubačić is an anarchist from the Balkans. Staughton Lynd is a lifelong pacifist, influenced by Marxism. They meet in dialogue in an effort to bring together the anarchist and Marxist traditions, to discuss the writing of history by those who make it, and to remind us of the idea that "my country is the world." Encompassing a Left libertarian perspective and an emphatically activist standpoint, these conversations are meant to be read in the clubs and affinity groups of the new Movement.

The authors accompany us on a journey through modern revolutions, direct actions, anti-globalist counter summits, Freedom Schools, Zapatista cooperatives, Haymarket and Petrograd, Hanoi and Belgrade, 'intentional' communities, wildcat strikes, early Protestant communities, Native American democratic practices, the Workers' Solidarity Club of Youngstown, occupied factories, self-organized councils and soviets, the lives of forgotten revolutionaries, Quaker meetings, antiwar movements, and prison rebellions. Neglected and forgotten moments of interracial self-activity are brought to light. The book invites the attention of readers who believe that a better world, on the other side of capitalism and state bureaucracy, may indeed be possible.

"There's no doubt that we've lost much of our history. It's also very clear that those in power in this country like it that way. Here's a book that shows us why. It demonstrates not only that another world is possible, but that it already exists, has existed, and shows an endless potential to burst through the artificial walls and divisions that currently imprison us. An exquisite contribution to the literature of human freedom, and coming not a moment too soon."
—David Graeber, author of *Fragments of an Anarchist Anthropology* and *Direct Action: An Ethnography*

"I have been in regular contact with Andrej Grubačić for many years, and have been most impressed by his searching intelligence, broad knowledge, lucid judgment, and penetrating commentary on contemporary affairs and their historical roots. He is an original thinker and dedicated activist, who brings deep understanding and outstanding personal qualities to everything he does."
—Noam Chomsky

Joe Hill: The IWW & the Making of a Revolutionary Workingclass Counterculture, Second Edition

Franklin Rosemont with an Introduction by David Roediger

ISBN: 978-1-62963-119-6
$29.95   656 pages

A monumental work, expansive in scope, covering the life, times, and culture of that most famous of the Wobblies—songwriter, poet, hobo, thinker, humorist, martyr—Joe Hill. It is a journey into the Wobbly culture that made Hill and the capitalist culture that killed him. Many aspects of the life and lore of Joe Hill receive their first and only discussion in IWW historian Franklin Rosemont's opus.

In great detail, the issues that Joe Hill raised and grappled with in his life: capitalism, white supremacy, gender, religion, wilderness, law, prison, and industrial unionism are shown in both the context of Hill's life and for their enduring relevance in the century since his death.

Collected too is Joe Hill's art, plus scores of other images featuring Hill-inspired art by IWW illustrators from Ralph Chaplin to Carlos Cortez, as well as contributions from many other labor artists.

As Rosemont suggests in this remarkable book, Joe Hill never really died. He lives in the minds of young (and old) rebels as long as his songs are sung, his ideas are circulated, and his political descendants keep fighting for a better day.

"Joe Hill has finally found a chronicler worthy of his revolutionary spirit, sense of humor, and poetic imagination."
—Robin D.G. Kelley, author of *Freedom Dreams*

"Rosemont's treatment of Joe Hill is passionate, polemical, and downright entertaining. What he gives us is an extended and detailed argument for considering both Hill and the IWW for their contributions toward creating an autonomous and uncompromising alternative culture."
—Gordon Simmons, *Labor Studies Journal*

"Magnificent, practical, irreverent and (as one might say) magisterial, written in a direct, passionate, sometimes funny, deeply searching style."
—Peter Linebaugh, author of *Stop, Thief!*

New Forms of Worker Organization: The Syndicalist and Autonomist Restoration of Class Struggle Unionism

Edited by Immanuel Ness
with a foreword by Staughton Lynd

ISBN: 978-1-60486-956-9
$24.95   336 pages

Bureaucratic labor unions are under assault. Most unions have surrendered the achievements of the mid-twentieth century, when the working class was a militant force for change throughout the world. Now trade unions seem incapable of defending, let alone advancing, workers' interests.

As unions implode and weaken, workers are independently forming their own unions, drawing on the tradition of syndicalism and autonomism—a resurgence of self-directed action that augurs a new period of class struggle throughout the world. In Africa, Asia, the Americas, and Europe, workers are rejecting leaders and forming authentic class-struggle unions rooted in sabotage, direct action, and striking to achieve concrete gains.

This is the first book to compile workers' struggles on a global basis, examining the formation and expansion of radical unions in the Global South and Global North. The tangible evidence marshaled in this book serves as a handbook for understanding the formidable obstacles and concrete opportunities for workers challenging neoliberal capitalism, even as the unions of the old decline and disappear.

Contributors include Au Loong-Yu, Bai Ruixue, Arup K. Sen, Shawn Hattingh, Piotr Bizyukov and Irina Olimpieva, Genese M. Sodikoff, Aviva Chomsky, Dario Bursztyn, Gabriel Kuhn, Erik Forman, Steven Manicastri, Arup Kumar Sen, and Jack Kirkpatrick.

"As the U.S. labor movement conducts its latest, frantic search for 'new ideas,' there is no better source of radical thinking on improved modes of union functioning than the diverse contributors to this timely collection. New Forms of Worker Organization *vividly describes what workers in Africa, Asia, South America, and Europe have done to make their unions more effective. Let's hope that these compelling case studies of rank-and-file struggle and bottom up change lead to more of the same where it's needed the most, among those of us 'born in the USA!'"*
—Steve Early, former organizer for the Communications Workers of America and author of *Save Our Unions: Dispatches from a Movement in Distress*

Abolish Work: "Abolish Restaurants" Plus "Work, Community, Politics, War"

Prole.info

ISBN: 978-1-60486-340-6
$9.95   96 pages

Finally available for the first time in a single book format, *Abolish Work* combines two influential and well-circulated pamphlets written from the frontlines of the class war. The texts from the anonymous workers at Prole.info offer cutting-edge class analysis and critiques of daily life accompanied by uncensored, innovative illustrations.

Moving from personal thoughts and interactions to large-scale political and economic forces, *Abolish Work* reads alternately like a worker's diary, a short story, a psychology of everyday life, a historical account, and an angry flyer someone would pass you on the street.

The classic "Abolish Restaurants" is an illustrated guide to the daily misery, stress, boredom, and alienation of restaurant work, as well as the ways in which restaurant workers fight against it. Drawing on a range of anti-capitalist ideas as well as a heaping plate of personal experience, it is part analysis and part call-to-arms. An additional piece, "Work, Community, Politics, War" is a comic book introduction to modern society, identifying both the oppressive and subversive tendencies that exist today in order to completely remake society.

"The entire booklet is enthralling, perhaps especially so if you don't already know what goes on behind the scenes for underpaid, non-unionized restaurant workers in the United States."
—Brittany Shoot, Change.org

"The stress of the dinner rush, the fights with co-workers, the split shifts, the lousy tippers, the aching backs . . . It is not just random individual misfortune. It is a functional and necessary part of a larger system that creates similar conditions everywhere. Capitalist society is built on class struggle, and Abolish Work *puts forward the perspective of one side in that struggle."*
—Mickey Z., PlanetGreen.com

Stop, Thief!
The Commons, Enclosures, and Resistance

Peter Linebaugh

ISBN: 978-1-60486-747-3
$21.95   304 pages

In this majestic tour de force, celebrated historian Peter Linebaugh takes aim at the thieves of land, the polluters of the seas, the ravagers of the forests, the despoilers of rivers, and the removers of mountaintops. Scarcely a society has existed on the face of the earth that has not had commoning at its heart. "Neither the state nor the market," say the planetary commoners. These essays kindle the embers of memory to ignite our future commons.

From Thomas Paine to the Luddites, from Karl Marx—who concluded his great study of capitalism with the enclosure of commons—to the practical dreamer William Morris—who made communism into a verb and advocated communizing industry and agriculture—to the 20th-century communist historian E.P. Thompson, Linebaugh brings to life the vital commonist tradition. He traces the red thread from the great revolt of commoners in 1381 to the enclosures of Ireland, and the American commons, where European immigrants who had been expelled from their commons met the immense commons of the native peoples and the underground African-American urban commons. Illuminating these struggles in this indispensable collection, Linebaugh reignites the ancient cry, "STOP, THIEF!"

"There is not a more important historian living today. Period."
—Robin D.G. Kelley, author of *Freedom Dreams: The Black Radical Imagination*

"E.P. Thompson, you may rest now. Linebaugh restores the dignity of the despised luddites with a poetic grace worthy of the master… [A] commonist manifesto for the 21st century."
—Mike Davis, author of *Planet of Slums*

"Peter Linebaugh's great act of historical imagination… takes the cliché of 'globalization' and makes it live. The local and the global are once again shown to be inseparable—as they are, at present, for the machine-breakers of the new world crisis."
—T.J. Clark, author of *Farewell to an Idea*

The Incomplete, True, Authentic, and Wonderful History of May Day

Peter Linebaugh

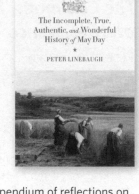

ISBN: 978-1-62963-107-3
$15.95   200 pages

"May Day is about affirmation, the love of life, and the start of spring, so it has to be about the beginning of the end of the capitalist system of exploitation, oppression, war, and overall misery, toil, and moil." So writes celebrated historian Peter Linebaugh in an essential compendium of reflections on the reviled, glorious, and voltaic occasion of May 1st.

It is a day that has made the rich and powerful cower in fear and caused Parliament to ban the Maypole—a magnificent and riotous day of rebirth, renewal, and refusal. These reflections on the Red and the Green—out of which arguably the only hope for the future lies—are populated by the likes of Native American anarcho-communist Lucy Parsons, the Dodge Revolutionary Union Movement, Karl Marx, José Martí, W.E.B. Du Bois, Rosa Luxemburg, SNCC, and countless others, both sentient and verdant. The book is a forceful reminder of the potentialities of the future, for the coming of a time when the powerful will fall, the commons restored, and a better world born anew.

"There is not a more important historian living today. Period."
—Robin D.G. Kelley, author of *Freedom Dreams: The Black Radical Imagination*

"E.P. Thompson, you may rest now. Linebaugh restores the dignity of the despised luddites with a poetic grace worthy of the master."
—Mike Davis, author of *Planet of Slums*

"Ideas can be beautiful too, and the ideas Peter Linebaugh provokes and maps in this history of liberty are dazzling reminders of what we have been and who we could be."
—Rebecca Solnit, author of *Storming the Gates of Paradise*

Why Work? Arguments for the Leisure Society

Edited by Freedom Press with an
Introduction by Nina Power

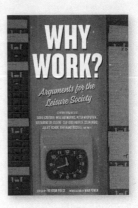

ISBN: 978-1-62963-576-7
$19.95   224 pages

Why Work? is a provocative collection of essays and
illustrations by writers and artists from the nineteenth
century through to today, dissecting "work," its form
under capitalism, and the possibilities for an alternative
society. It asks: Why do some of us still work until we drop in an age of vast
automated production, while others starve for lack of work? Where is the leisure
society that was promised?

Edited by Freedom Press, this collection includes contributions from luminaries
of the past such as William Morris and Bertrand Russell, contemporary theorists
such as David Graeber and Juliet Schor, and illustrated examinations of workplace
potentials and pitfalls from Clifford Harper and Prole.info.

A History of Pan-African Revolt

C.L.R. James with an Introduction by Robin D.G. Kelley

ISBN: 978-1-60486-095-5
$16.95   160 pages

Originally published in England in 1938 (the same year as his magnum opus *The Black Jacobins*) and expanded in 1969, this work remains the classic account of global black resistance. Robin D.G. Kelley's substantial introduction contextualizes the work in the history and ferment of the times, and explores its ongoing relevance today.

"*A History of Pan-African Revolt* is one of those rare books that continues to strike a chord of urgency, even half a century after it was first published. Time and time again, its lessons have proven to be valuable and relevant for understanding liberation movements in Africa and the diaspora. Each generation who has had the opportunity to read this small book finds new insights, new lessons, new visions for their own age . . . . No piece of literature can substitute for a crystal ball, and only religious fundamentalists believe that a book can provide comprehensive answers to all questions. But if nothing else, *A History of Pan-African Revolt* leaves us with two incontrovertible facts. First, as long as black people are denied freedom, humanity and a decent standard of living, they will continue to revolt. Second, unless these revolts involve the ordinary masses and take place on their own terms, they have no hope of succeeding." —Robin D.G. Kelley, from the Introduction

"I wish my readers to understand the history of Pan-African Revolt. They fought, they suffered—they are still fighting. Once we understand that, we can tackle our problems with the necessary mental equilibrium." —C.L.R. James

"*Kudos for reissuing C.L.R. James's pioneering work on black resistance. Many brilliant embryonic ideas articulated in* A History of Pan-African Revolt *twenty years later became the way to study black social movements. Robin Kelley's introduction superbly situates James and his thought in the world of Pan-African and Marxist intellectuals.*" —Sundiata Cha-Jua, Penn State University

"*A mine of ideas advancing far ahead of its time.*" —Walter Rodney

"*When one looks back over the last twenty years to those men who were most far-sighted, who first began to tease out the muddle of ideology in our times, who were at the same time Marxists with a hard theoretical basis, and close students of society, humanists with a tremendous response to and understanding of human culture, Comrade James is one of the first one thinks of.*" —E.P. Thompson